*When I go out on stage and feel frightened
of the darkness glittering with eyes, I think
of him.*

TOM HOLLANDER

*Someone once asked what he did for a living.
'I stand up,' he said, 'I put on make-up, and
I shout in the evenings.'*

DANIEL CRAIG

PREFACE

*There are no hard distinctions between what
is real and what is unreal, nor between what is
true and what is false. A thing is not necessarily
either true or false; it can be both true and false.*

HAROLD PINTER

When Michael Gambon's memory began to fade, he found it increasingly difficult to remember his lines. Ultimately, the job fell to me to be his 'earwig', which from 2010 I did for nine years, giving him his lines through an earpiece. This allowed me to see and hear him deliver some outstanding performances, great jokes and stories, for which he was well known both publicly and privately.

Over the past few years, since he died, I have been in touch with many actors, directors and writers who worked alongside him, as well as those who interviewed him over the years and others who have generously contributed anecdotes about his impact on their lives. The collection of these stories is the book you hold in your hands.

These are not just thespy tittle-tattle but examples of the

mischief, kindness, brilliance and bravura which enshrine the volcanic force of nature that was Michael, changing everyone he touched and creating mayhem, laughter and breathtaking performances in his path.

Alongside this, I saw and felt his frustration at having to rely on someone else to remind him of his lines, however well hidden the effort may have been, and witnessed his despair at having to retire from his sanctuary, the stage. I witnessed his fury at his declining powers, his raging and his attempts to disguise this by playing the fool. Luckily the warmth of the laughter, the games, the pranks and the incredible joy he brought to us remain in interviews on film. This book, or Festschrift, is my tribute to a consummate mythmaker, a spinner of yarns, a preposterous bender of truths and a legend so greatly admired by so many.

1

'Everyone thought I played the banjo'

To begin at the beginning. Michael John Gambon was born in Cabra, Dublin, Ireland, on 19 October 1940. He was the eldest of three children (a sister Theresa and brother John) delivered to Edward and Mary Gambon. He would say, with utter conviction: 'Gambon is quite a common name in County Wexford in Ireland. It must be to do with the Spanish Armada, which went aground along the coast of Ireland ... My dad was dark-looking.' Michael had been reliably informed of the derivation of the name by a friend and fellow Irishman: 'He's a bit of a genealogist,' he remarked with pride.

Whatever the mythology, history confirms that his father moved to London after the war to find work. During the war, he was a reserve policeman. Michael's earliest memories of Ireland were indelibly stored in his mind because every Sunday, with almost liturgical precision, a hilarious scenario took place in the dining room of his family home.

As he recounted the tale, Michael always adopted an incredibly exaggerated Oirish oul' Dubs accent for his auld mammie.

Imagine a sweet, demure little lady and her sister, both meek, pious and extremely genteel:

> Every Sunday at our house, there'd be an enormous slap-up do for Father Patrick, the old priest, after mass, by which time he'd've worked himself into a lather of appetite, a fierce appetite. He had, all before lunch: sausages, potatoes, bacon, fresh bread, fruit cake, cheese, the lot, and the whole time that old priest, he'd be eyeing up this lovely antique Irish dresser, my mammie's pride and joy, and kept up a running monologue between helping himself to generous mouthfuls – mounds – of food.

Michael mimed having a full mouth and gesticulating while greedily shovelling in more food and becoming more inarticulate as the story went on.

> 'Now, Mary, dat, over der, let me tell you, is a very fine dresser and, to my mind, would look marvellous in the vestry; yes, Mary, you'd be doing the church a very great service. Yes, that would be a wonderful asset to the vestry, Mary, so it would.'
>
> And my mammie, smiling sweetly and meekly, respectfully bobbing up and down, all the while as though she was either stone deaf or a complete imbecile, would say by way of answer:
>
> 'Oh, here you go, you must be famished. Faather, won't you have more bread, another slice of fruit cake, perhaps, another cup of tea? You will, will you, Faather?' Completely evading an answer to the question.
>
> Anyways, this dance continued until he'd eaten enough for six of us, then he'd heave himself to his feet and start the slow preparation to leave. Up jumped the sisters to see him off:

'Bye, Faather, bye, see ya next week, God willing.' They'd be waving and crossing themselves on the doorstep, checking he'd gone down the road waiting for his final 'God bless you both' and 'Mary, now don't you be forgettin' about dat fine dresser now,' he'd call back over his shoulder.

No sooner than you could say three Hail Marys, that front door would slam, and in unison with voices fiercer than banshees, and without drawing breath – they'd exclaim in unison:

'Dat auld fecker, he's not getting his filthy mitts on dat der dresser. He's about to be diddling us out of de furniture. I'm going to be buried in it, so I am.'

This ritual went on every Sunday till we left – him trying to diddle me old mammie out of the dresser, that fecker. I am happy to say he never got it. And she always planned to be buried in it.

I was never told if this wish was ever granted to her.

When Michael was five, they all moved to London and joined their daddy there. His father worked in a factory, and the Gambons moved into a flat in Camden Town, north London, where a large Irish community already existed. Michael's schooldays mainly consisted of him mucking about with the other boys, smoking, taking radios apart, riding his bike and causing havoc.

I used to carry around an empty banjo case. Everyone thought I played the banjo. My best friend was a quiet Indian boy called Kevin who lived nearby; we spent most of our time together just inventing stories. We would tell each other what our daddies did and what our mammies did. All lies, and we'd know they were lies. Children know. You enter a pact, a game.

I'd say my father had gone to Africa. We spent our Saturdays breaking into London Zoo and fishing in the canal.

Then we would take the spokes out of a bicycle wheel, tie a burlap sack to the rim, put half a loaf of bread in the centre, and lower it into the water. The gudgeon fish would feed; you'd slowly raise the sack.

Michael's nimble fingers mime the scene, rendering his words superfluous – they would flog the trapped fish as bait.

One day, Michael revealed, almost as an afterthought, that he fell in. And in those days, inner-city children never learned to swim.

I clearly remember looking up through the water at the sky and seeing all the colours of blue. A man dived in from the bridge – I never saw him again – and dragged me out. I'd certainly be dead otherwise. I don't remember any fear, I just remember being lifted out into the air, and placed onto the bank. I stayed there till I dried. Then we went to the zoo, went home, and never told anyone.

He went to school at St Aloysius' in Highgate, which led to his first public performance, aged eleven or twelve, as an altar boy. He took this role extremely seriously, mainly because of the dressing up. With great pride, he said that he had learned the entire text in Latin and served at six o'clock mass every morning. He adored the vestments and, of course, the ceremonial and performative aspect. Swinging the incense and holding the chalice during Holy Communion and stuff – he loved all that. And he would change the words during the mass, reciting solemnly: 'me Mexican cowboy, me Mexican cowboy' (instead of the correct

Latin phrase – 'mea maxima culpa' – which means 'through my most grievous fault').

Then, around the age of thirteen, he became a Sea Cadet in the First City of London Sea Cadet Corps, the St Clement Danes unit. On the day of the coronation in 1953, he told me how proud he was, standing there in full kit, gaiters, rifle, bayonet.

Another uniform. Another costume. Another public performance.

In 1955 his parents moved to near Crayford in Kent. He left school and took the first job he could in a factory learning how to mend things, sweeping floors, making tea and watching as the older men made radios and television sets. Not long after, he moved to a nearby tool-and-die works, partly, he remembered, because he was given a white coat there. This is a powerful theme that runs through his life. Clothes mattered to Michael; he was always hugely interested in costumes and enjoyed wearing elegant clothes. This is not altogether surprising as Michael said his mother was a seamstress for Norman Hartnell (the Queen's dressmaker) and would make their clothes from off-cuts. This possibly accounts for his love of bespoke suits from Savile Row. He was always extremely critical of how something was cut and made.

His proud boast to me was that he owned around a hundred suits and several hundred pairs of shoes, mostly handmade because of his enormous feet, and some bespoke overcoats. Michael always demanded that the costume department give him the suits made for him in any production as part of his deal. He had an extremely refined aesthetic, apart from his taste in food, which remained 'An excellent ole fry-up, chips and extra puddings with custard or cream – lashings of it.'

About the clothes he freely admitted, 'It's just the

getting-something-for-nothing part of me; I can't resist it,' he'd say with a nod and a wink. 'Good stuff, this,' he'd add as he examined a beautiful tweed suit or coat: 'Great schmutter! I just had to have all those clothes because they were beautiful and, of course, free.'

In terms of the education he received, he was always very clear about this as well as his powerful ability at make-believe.

'I was hopeless at school. I just spent my time staring out of the window, dreaming. I was always pretending to be someone else.' He later said, 'I think it helps that I'm Irish and it helps that I'm a dreamer – Celtic twilight, and all that. Acting is very sophisticated lying, isn't it? Highly skilled lying.'

Chugging on a succession of Benson & Hedges and drinking tea (three sugars), he would talk of his youth as we sat between takes on various productions, smiling to himself as he looked back over his early, very different life.

In 1956, Michael passed an entrance exam for the engineering firm Vickers-Armstrongs, who made everything from shotguns to sewing machines. Thus began his lifelong fascination with everything mechanical, his passion for antique firearms, craftsmanship and precision.

Looking at Michael, it seemed at odds with his physique, with his long, almost simian arms and massive hands, which he used gracefully to articulate a phrase, conjure an attitude when telling a joke, or even to chain-light another cigarette. It was fascinating seeing him handle the intricate mechanisms of watches and listening to how he could rebuild and fix them. He loved handmade analogue watches and owned an amazing collection.

On some films he might be found round the corner from the location, in the nearest garage, under the bonnet of a car, 'offering a helping hand' to the delighted mechanics. He knew how to replace gearboxes and loved 'tinkering' with engines, as he put it. He owned many cars; they were one of his greatest passions, along with his collections of analogue watches and guns. Exquisite cars, I was told: 'Ferraris, Lamborghinis, sports cars – posh cars – too posh for you to go in, Mugwhay, I'm afraid,' he would say very seriously. ('Mugwhay' was his nickname for me.)

Talking of his hands, he said that he was having lunch with friends at Wheelers, the bohemian haunt and oyster bar in Old Compton Street, Soho, when Francis Bacon came by his table and remarked that he would love to paint them. Quick as a flash, Michael pushed his plate aside, cleared the table, took out his pen and drew around his hands on the tablecloth. Then he presented the cloth to Bacon, saying: 'There ya go!'

One of his obsessions was beautiful handguns and he started collecting them around the age of twelve.

I've always liked guns as works of art, as antiques … My dad used to bring them home from junk shops. You could buy them for next to nothing. He'd wander around these old markets in north London and bring them home on a Saturday morning, guns, swords and rusty old bits of junk, and we'd hang them on my bedroom wall.

Michael's lifelong passion for restoring antique guns and pistols, particularly their intricate inlay, became part of his own mythology. As Tom Hollander would recall, 'He loved to speak of his other lives. How as a young apprentice at Holland & Holland, he worked with his long craftsman's fingers on a gun for Khrushchev. How a piece of his treasured antique gun collection (merely a good fake) was on loan to a museum in Canada.'

So perfected was his technique in the art of inlay that often he would boast that experts mistook his work for the original article. Astonishingly, this skill was completely self-taught:

> I've taught myself inlay, an incredibly complex eighteenth-century craft. Through years of painstaking practice, I've developed my own technique, perfecting the delicate, intricate work of rococo scrolls intertwined with shells, floral elements like acanthus leaves – a truly breathtakingly beautiful art form. Most of what I read in books about it was nonsense, frankly. It was mostly trial and error, and now I can make things that people genuinely believe are authentic and from the eighteenth century. It's a bit like acting, isn't it? Creating an illusion, pulling the wool over people's eyes, faking things.

Of course, although Michael loved to say acting was just being a child and 'mucking about on stage', the truth is that he took it deadly seriously. He was a finely detailed craftsman and a brilliant, intuitive performer with a superb command of his body and voice. On stage, he was the consummate master of the specific move or gesture. He has been described by many actors and directors as a magical being, mythical, part clown, part mercurial creature.

His interest in acting was really sparked when, sometime around his sixteenth birthday, he and a friend came out of a cinema where they had been watching a film starring his hero, Marlon Brando. As they walked home, they saw a sign outside a local amateur theatre called the Erith Playhouse, where he read that they needed backstage help. The Erith was a tiny theatre on the high street near his home.

Curious, he entered that world, where, with his aptitude for making things, he started helping to build sets as a volunteer.

Why had he stepped inside the door? He told me he felt drawn, that he thought theatre might be like cinema, and because he so idolised the great Marlon Brando; his mate told him that's where they did the acting stuff, and so it began.

First, with carpentry, then the moment he stepped on stage, he said, 'It was electrifying, VAROOM – I thought, Jesus, this is for me. This is my family, my tribe; I want to be an actor.'

Of course, he also had to keep this secret from his mates at work and in the pub as he was afraid of being teased and told it was effete and that dressing up was only for queers.

Too late: he was intoxicated, and in 1957, after buying some theatre magazines, he saw an ad in one called *Amateur Stage* for the celebrated Unity Theatre, which he remembered playing outside in the street as a small child when he lived in north London. The Unity Theatre started in the 1930s as agitprop street theatre and grew into a venue that championed left-wing ideas and artistic expression. It was also the first theatre in England to stage a play by Bertold Brecht. Michael always stridently denied he knew anything about their politics, but there is an interesting contradiction here.

In an interview he gave to the theatre critic Michael Billington at the HighTide Festival in Halesworth in 2014, he claimed that his father had put him in touch with the Unity as 'he was a bit of communist'.

So, he now commuted from Kent and his work at Vickers in the factory by day and performed in amateur theatricals by night.

2

'*I wanted to be behind the curtain*'

During this period, he also worked with another amateur theatre company, the Tower Theatre in Islington. This got him his first paid job, at the Royal Court, a Sunday night play, *The Sea at Dauphin* by Derek Walcott, which gives the audience a glimpse into the tough lives of the fishermen and villagers of the Caribbean. Michael was the only white actor in a company of black actors, but, as far as he was concerned, the time had come to announce himself to the world:

> I was totally stagestruck and kept finding excuses to go in and out of the stage door – I couldn't help myself. I'd go out, walk around Sloane Square and go in again, hoping someone would see me through the stage door. It sounds utterly mad, but I still am stagestruck; that's what I've always been. To tell the truth, I became an actor because I wanted to be behind the curtain, in that secret world of the curtain, the stage door, the backstage – with the audience out there. I like to retain the mystery, the magic, the other world.

Michael was a complicated man, often self-deprecating, with the imposter syndrome running through him as indelibly as lettering in a stick of rock. Even into his late seventies he was scared he'd be revealed as a fraud – a fake – and sent back to the factory. He doubted his ability to articulate his ideas about how he came to make his choices. One thing he was clear about above everything else, however:

> That's the job, to make people believe it. It's got to be. You can't fudge it. I never thought I would do this well, though. I thought it would eventually come to an end ... It would stop, and I would do something else. Like a blink of an eye, you wake up after forty years and think, I've done this all my life. I've earned a living, I've got a knighthood. This is remarkable, isn't it? I have a great big country house. I have a Mercedes, a Ferrari; I have forty suits, handmade shoes; I have antiques. And I can pinch myself and think, it's all from being an actor. And I never thought when I started being a professional actor that it would last. I thought it was a phase you go through.

He often spoke about fakery, about lying, about the virtues of obstinacy and of telling stories. This was another theme that ran through his life – inventing things rather than revealing anything much about himself. Of course, by doing this he revealed much more than he ever imagined. He was an instinctive rather than a technical actor: 'I admire technical facility in others, but I'm a hit-and-miss merchant. I'm afraid I do my own sort of thing.' Of course that is incredibly powerful. Michael's enormous ability was to express subtlety and intensity of feeling through minute movements or vocal inflections. He demonstrated this by taking the central character in Harold Pinter's *The Caretaker*, who is often asked, 'Welsh, aren't you?' To which he replies, 'It's a bit hard, like, to set your mind back.'

What is so moving about Michael's ability is that, as he says these lines, he becomes deflated and defeated, and there is an awful sense of pathos, a mournful loss and longing. It winds you, knocks you sideways and leaves you breathless. He has a tremendous access to his emotion, and he always wants to keep things in check. He can access the complexity in very simple people.

'We're all deeply complex,' he told one journalist in an interview, 'all that much' – and he would hold his hands together – 'on the surface and that much' – he would then stretch his hands wide apart – 'beneath: the subtext of life.'

That is a brilliant summation of his approach; for Michael, that was acting: 'it's like diving into the rich depths of existence and resurfacing with some precious pearls'. His ability to see into the heart of the human condition and reveal it for an audience in ways they could both believe and recognise.

Sir Peter Hall said: 'He can switch off different areas of his personality and remake himself. I think that's called genius. How does he do it? I don't suppose he can tell you. Most actors bring the part to themselves. In some curious way, Michael takes himself to the part. Fate gave him genius, but he uses it as a craftsman.'

He hated being questioned about himself in interviews, being revealed to the public without a script. He used to say: 'I always want to say to critics, "Why don't you mind your own fucking business?"'

He wanted to be an actor in the same way that other men were bus drivers or cabbies, doing their jobs without constantly being interrogated. Private, secretive, mysterious in his way, like Walter Mitty.

Rupert Goold brilliantly observed with a naturalist's precision that 'his natural habitat [was] the backstage corridors and
wings of a theatre, wreathed in smoke and nervy camaraderie'.
Telling stories was, of course, a brilliant way of deflecting questions about his personal life. Michael would always quote Paul
Scofield's view that when he was not acting in a play he didn't
really exist.

Michael said:

It's only when I'm acting in a play that I've got something to
say about the world. And then why should I talk, when people
can come to see it? . . . I just plod on and try to keep my mouth
shut, mind my own business. I find the whole thing about
people's lives . . . I can't understand it. I'm always astonished
that people want to know anything about me.

Matthew Warchus gave brilliant insight, having worked with
Michael on numerous occasions, when he told an interviewer:

He's very private. I know other actors who are like that and
it's connected to the acting. In the theatre, among actors,
directors, writers, the skill – talent – is a by-product of social
dysfunction: outsiders, shy people . . . They're channelling
something that would otherwise be extremely problematic . . .
Part of what you're doing in rehearsal is building the only
partially visible and the invisible. A great performance gives
a glimpse of something, so that you feel there's a huge story
behind the character. And there's an enormous story behind
Michael. But I think there's a secret part of actors that is best
to leave secret.

Michael was an incredible observer and always curious about how people worked: the mechanics of a person, literally what made them tick. And he was especially fascinated by and drawn to those individuals who seemed 'other' – outsiders, loners, slightly apart, eccentric or 'quirky'. A typical example of this was when he was having supper at the Savoy Grill one night with the director John Dexter. As they were leaving, John stopped to talk to a group of musicians at a table and conversed with the conductor. And Michael said:

> A little man was sitting there, and I was standing there waiting for John to finish. This little man looked up and said, 'Hello,' and not knowing who he was, I said, 'Oh, hello. Have you been working?' and he said, 'Oh yes,' and I said, 'What do you do?' and he said, with a European accent: 'I play the piano.' And so I started waving my hands in the air and said, 'People say I should play the piano because of my long fingers.' The pianist replied, 'Well, they are wrong because yours are very long, and you need strength in your fingers to play.'
>
> 'Oh,' I said, 'that's nice. What's your name?' And he said, 'Arthur Rubinstein.'

Michael loved music and was extremely accomplished on the guitar, but he loved to share one of his stories which shifted almost daily between the version in which he could play the banjo and the one in which he only made it seem as if he could.

One Saturday night he stood in for a band member on his banjo. The band was called Big Bill Brunskill and his Downtown Stompers. But, alas, Michael only knew four chords, all out of tune, so when they came to play the opening number, it was a disaster. 'A travesty, but worse still, I didn't get paid. Bloody cheek!' he would always add in a bewildered and outraged tone.

Every summer, the family made a pilgrimage to Ireland to be with their relatives in Dublin. Michael's cousin Gerry Maguire, who moved to County Donegal later in life, said that Michael played tenor banjo in a jazz band and that they used to drive around in a hearse limo.

At one time, Michael told me he was a serious classical guitarist and had lessons with an equally serious Russian. On one occasion he met one of his heroes, the brilliant Julian Bream, perhaps the most famous classical guitarist of his generation, at a lunch party with friends in Dorset. Michael thought Julian Bream was a god, and he was in awe of his talent.

In 1962, Hilton Edwards and Micheál Mac Liammóir, the celebrated actor-managers of the Gate Theatre in Dublin, received a letter and résumé from a young actor. Later Michael confessed:

I was a terrible liar. I wrote a letter to Hilton Edwards and said I was flying to New York and passing through Dublin. Could I come and see him? So I went to Dublin and he said, 'What have you played?' and I told him I'd played Marchbanks in the West End. He didn't even question it. He said, 'Well, I can't offer you any good parts but would you play the Second Gentleman of Cyprus [in *Othello*]?' To say that to a man who's just played Marchbanks in the West End, he must have known I was bullshitting. I said 'Yes, I would love to.' Then he said, rehearsals would start on October 1st, and that was it. I did that and we played in the Dublin Theatre Festival and then we did a European tour.

In 1963 Michael came to London to understudy for Bob Todd at the Mermaid Theatre. Spike Milligan was playing the lead in *The Bedsitting Room*. One night, Bob asked Michael to go on for him and gave him a pound on the condition that he kept his mouth shut:

He said he was ill. But really, he wanted a night off because he had been offered a day's filming with the BBC. I had to stand on the top of a stepladder. I was wearing army boots, a Nazi steel helmet and a string vest, and I sang a song about washing powder:

'When I was a young man, my vest was always dirty ...'

And that was my West End debut.

3

Early days of acting training and meeting 'Sir'

Michael spoke about the early days of his acting training and meeting Olivier: for him, Laurence Olivier was always 'Sir'.

> I managed to get in an acting course at the Royal Court, which was run by Bill Gaskill and George Devine. It was an advanced improvisation class ... Improvisation and mask work. I went there for six months. Then Bill Gaskill was appointed an associate director of the new National Theatre, which was about to open, and so I managed to get an audition.

He had read that Laurence Olivier was starting a company and auditioning actors at the Old Vic: 'I didn't know much about it, but I decided to give it a try.'

> I was so green about the theatre and the history of the theatre and about him that I did Richard III for him for the audition ... When I look back on it now, I shake with embarrassment ...

He said, 'What are you going to do?' I said, 'Richard III.' He said, 'Which part?' I said, 'Richard III.' He said, 'I know. Which part?' He was fooling. He said, 'Which part? Catesby? Buckingham?' I said, 'No. Richard III.' He said, 'The king?' I said, 'Yes.' He said, 'You have the fucking cheek.' Then I was genuinely frightened. I said, 'Oh, I'm sorry.' He said, 'No, no: you do it.' I immediately started. He said, 'No, no. You're standing too close to me. You can't start doing that famous part leaning over me.' He was sitting at a table. 'You've got to walk away from me. I've got to see you in full perspective. Go to the back of the hall and do it there.' So I went up the hall. There were columns holding the roof up. I got to the last one. I dived for the column. I don't know what came over me. I spun round and started the speech, but as I went around, I ripped the whole of my hand. A nail in the column went straight through – blood, pfff! He said, 'No. Stop, stop. You're not dying, are you? What's happened? We have to get a doctor. Where's a doctor?' He gave me his handkerchief. He wrapped my hand. 'I'll do it now,' I said. He said, 'No, no. This is appalling.' I said, 'But I have to do the audition.' He said, 'You go away and we'll be in touch with you.'

As he'd bunked off work, he went back to the engineering factory in Islington where he was working. At four that afternoon he was bent over his lathe, working as best he could with a heavily bandaged hand, when he was called to the phone. It was the Old Vic.

Michael loved enacting this bit, miming his hyper-intense focus over the lathe with his tongue stuck out for added effect.

It's not easy talking on the phone. One, there's the noise of the machinery. Two, I must keep my voice down 'cause I'm cockney at work and posh with theatre people. But they offer me a job, spear carrying, starting immediately. I go back to my workbench, heart beating in my chest, pack my tool case, start to go. The foreman comes up, says, 'Oi, where you off to?'

'I've got bad news,' I say, 'I've got to go.' He says, 'Why are you taking your toolbox?' I say, 'I can't tell you, it's very bad news, it's very bad news, might need it.' And I never went back there. Home on the bus, heart still thumping away. A whole new world ahead. We tend to forget what it felt like in the beginning.

He was with the Old Vic from 1963 to 1967. The next episode took place shortly after Michael had joined the company at the age of twenty-three. Fresh in his memory was the challenging and humiliating episode of his audition and he was determined to impress the great man. At this moment they were preparing Sir Laurence Olivier's famous production of *Hamlet* starring Peter O'Toole, just back from filming *Lawrence of Arabia*.

Michael was a spear carrier, sharing a job with a young Welsh actor, Anthony Hopkins, which was to lift Hamlet (O'Toole) from Ophelia's grave, an unbelievable honour for them. O'Toole, with his golden hair and dazzling looks, was a god. Michael was to lift his upper body under his arms and Anthony his legs.

Most mornings Michael would arrive at the Old Vic an hour early to give himself time to go down to the canteen in the basement, have a cup of tea and read the newspaper. Once, as he sat quietly doing this, he became acutely aware that someone was watching him intently.

'There were only two people in this vast canteen. Both had a

cup of tea. Every other table was vacant. And now sitting opposite me was the great man [Sir Laurence] staring at me through
his big dark glasses.'

Michael was anxious, starstruck and paralysed, fixed in the
full beam of his famous gaze.

Sir Laurence didn't remember who the fuck I was. As it
happened, a leather wallet lay on the table. Embossed on
the surface in big gold letters was the word NORGE. It was
the only thing I could focus on, and after the last occasion, I
wanted to make an impression. 'Norge,' I blurted out, stating
the obvious and pointing.

'What are you talking about?' he replied, a hint of irritation
in his voice, and clearly confused.

'The wallet,' I explained. 'It says "Norge". Like on
Norwegian stamps.' An idea, however bizarre, sparked in my
mind and, grasping for a connection, I added:

'When you played Hamlet at Elsinore? Did–did–did the
grateful people of Norway give you that wallet as a gift?'

A long silence followed. Then, his face hardening, he
said, 'Listen, you moron, I haven't the faintest fucking clue
what you are blithering on about. That is not my wallet, and
Elsinore isn't in fucking Norway, it's in Denmark. Good
morning to you.' He stood, turned on his heel and left me
baffled and staring at the wallet.

I was so nervous, I never knew quite what to say to him. I
was always tongue-tied. Something about being in the presence of greatness.

Years later, when John Dexter took him to visit the Oliviers
for dinner at their country cottage in Sussex, Michael recalled: 'I

just couldn't call him Larry, he was Sir. At a certain point during dinner, he started talking about Leontes in *The Winter's Tale*, and quoted the line, "There's a spider in my cup." "Do you remember that bit?" he asked. "'There's a spider in my goblet', something like that." I said, "Oh, yes," and just smiled and nodded like a mechanical toy dog – Olivier just stared at me as if I was an utter moron until Lady Olivier asked me if I liked trifle and I nodded gratefully and after that just sat there eating mountains of trifle so I couldn't answer any more questions. Humiliating.'

Apparently, Anthony Hopkins had once also suffered from this nervousness and had lied to Olivier about where he was born and blurted out that he had been born in Scotland instead of Bridgend, Wales. Michael said that was the effect he had on the company. 'We were all terrified of him; even Maggie [Smith] was terrified of him!'

TIM ACKROYD

When we were working together at the RSC in the early eighties, [on the first day] I went over to see Michael and said, 'Peter O'Toole sends his love,' and Michael said, 'Oh, that's very kind of him. Peter O'Toole, he threw me out of his dressing room.'

And I said, *What?*

He said:

He threw me out of his dressing room. *Hamlet* opened the National Theatre at the Old Vic in 1963. I was carrying a spear, and it was right at the top of the stage with Tony Hopkins. We were very keen then and used to arrive five hours before the start, to put on our false beards and our armour. Just imagine: Olivier was directing; they were fucking gods. They were gods. And so, *Hamlet* had just opened. It had been three or four days, and there was about half an hour before curtain-up, and over the PA came a voice: 'Michael Gambon to Mr O'Toole's dressing room, Michael Gambon to Mr O'Toole's dressing room.'

And Tony Hopkins said, 'What have you done?' I said, 'I don't know!'

So anyway, I picked up my spear and went all the way down the steps in my armour and knocked on the door to number one dressing room. There was no answer and so I knocked again. No answer. So I opened it slightly and I looked in. There, sitting in front of his mirror with his black tights on, was Peter O'Toole putting his make-up on, and he looked at me and said, 'Who the fuck are you?' and I said, 'I'm Michael Gambon,' and he said, 'Fuck off!'

And I went out, shut the door, and stood outside with my spear. The company manager came along, and she said, 'What are you doing there?'

'Well, I'm Gambon, the boy,' and she said, 'Oh, yes, that's right, he wants to see you.'

'Well, he just told me to go away,' and she said, 'Oh, you come on in with me.'

She knocked, took me in and left me there. I was just standing there with my spear. He says nothing, just carries on making up, smoking and after about five minutes he looks at me in the mirror and says, 'Now, are you the boy that picked me out of Ophelia's grave?' And I said, 'Yes, I am,' and he stood up, and he was a big man, and he drew his dagger, and said, 'You are going to be the first fucking actor to die on a London stage, because I am going to kill you.'

And I was 'Err . . .' And he said, 'You are a c—t, look, I've just come back from Cambodia [where he had been filming *Lord Jim*], and I've got six fucking injections in my arm, and if you pick me up with those gorilla's hands, I kid you not I am going to kill you, I am going to kill you tonight. What are you?'

I said, 'I'm a c—t,' and he said, 'You are! What a c—t,' and he sat down again and slammed his dagger down. I was shaking by then, and I said, 'Shall I go?' And he said, 'NO!' and I said, 'But it's five minutes to curtain-up,' and he said, 'I don't care about that – they can't start the play without me, I'm playing fucking Hamlet!' He says, 'Right! Now, we're going to work on this, right – put your spear there, and I'm going to lie down on the floor, and you're going to pick me up with those fucking gorilla hands of yours, but gently, otherwise...' and I said, 'You're going to kill me,' and he growled, 'Yes, I am.'

And he lay down. I slowly started leaning over, putting my hands on him, and picking him up very gently. As I lifted him, I said, 'I'm picking you out of the grave. I'm picking you up out of Ophelia's grave, out of the grave.'

Once up, he towered over me and said, 'You do it like that and you're the best fucking actor in the world! I'm gonna put you in my next film.' He said, 'You are fantastic!' and I said, 'Well, shall I go now?' and he said, 'No,' and I said, 'But it's beginners.' And he said, 'Forget beginners, forget the audience, forget fucking Olivier, just let me put my make-up on, no, don't go, you're a good boy. Go and get yourself a beer.' So, I got myself a beer out of his fridge and I stood there. It was hard as the helmet kept closing, and there was silence, and he said nothing, so I said, 'Er ...' And he said, 'What?!' and I said, 'Did you enjoy making *Lawrence*?' And he said, 'NO! I fucking hated it!'

Then I said, 'Did you, um . . . Did it take you long?'

And he said, 'Too fucking long,' and finally I said, 'Was it hot out there with all that sand?' and he stood up and grabbed me and kicked me out of the dressing room.

I arrived in the wings, and there was Tony Hopkins, and he said, 'What happened?' I looked at Tony, and I said, 'Well, he thinks I'm doing all right, really; he's going to put me in his next film!'

———————

Michael loved talking about the wild nights. The legendary wild nights at the Buckstone Club with Peter O'Toole, Albert Finney, Tim Ackroyd, Richard Harris and Michael Caine. The club was situated in a basement on Suffolk Street, behind the stage door of the Haymarket Theatre. Ronnie Corbett served drinks at the Buckstone Club between acting jobs.

They would go there every night. It was an actors' club, members only, and one of their challenges was that they had to go around the room without touching the floor, using the tops of the chairs and the bar, with each circuit becoming increasingly precarious as they got more drunk. He was always very nostalgic about those glorious years with dazzling talent like Nicol Williamson and claimed that he spent too much time lamenting the past; he lived in the past too much.

He also talked about acting being a compulsion. That actors have a built-in desire to be somebody else. To tell lies, to make up stories, to show off. In his opinion, they were in the main 'basically, big-headed bastards'.

There were those actors who for Michael remained sacred and Michael's admiration for Sir Ralph Richardson was also profound. He once said that, for Richardson, 'acting was like being in a dream', a sentiment he wholeheartedly agreed with. Their bond was strong, and with him Michael felt he had found a kindred spirit.

Richardson always felt relaxed, and Michael used to claim that they could talk about non-actory things. Sir Ralph loved motorbikes and would famously ride his bike through Hyde Park with a parrot on his shoulder. Most importantly, Richardson and Michael shared the same obsession with clocks and watches and were able to talk together endlessly about horology.

There is also a story about Michael having given Richardson a present after a play, a beautiful inlaid box which he had spent a great deal of time making for him, knowing of his huge appreciation of exquisite objects. Sir Ralph received his gift after the show in his dressing room which was cluttered and crowded with all kinds of paraphernalia (including his parrot), and rapturously applauded Michael's craftsmanship, before asking him to sit as he had a vitally important gift to offer him in return. After several minutes of rummaging and rifling around in a drawer in his dressing table, he produced an old piece of exquisite Indian paisley material wrapped around a large pill. It was black and looked more like a horse pill than anything else, and manky at that. He lifted it towards Michael with reverence and held it out to him. Michael stared at it suspiciously until he was commanded to swallow it – immediately.

Then he handed him a whisky tumbler and watched Michael swallow the enormous pill – like something from *Alice in Wonderland*.

'Now you shall from henceforth be known to the world as "the Great Gambon". You have taken the magical pill, and your performances will be marvellous. Next, you must hold this magical stone to keep in your pocket to ward off malignant spirits and help keep you grounded.'

Michael once showed me the stone, but I couldn't hold it unless I wanted to risk becoming an actress. We both agreed it was probably safest left to him alone.

Michael kept the magical stone in his pocket to ward off evil spirits. He and Richardson only worked together once, and Michael said that the play was a disaster, and that Sir Ralph had only decided to do it because there was an opening scene with him doing some needlework. Of course, Michael only did it to be with Sir Ralph. This was the beginning of a long friendship, and thereafter they often met at the National Theatre to chat and to discuss plays.

Michael staunchly believed that working with great actors rubbed off simply by watching them in action because you quickly learned that there was no secret to acting. 'They stand in the wings the way you do. We all used to watch Sir Laurence like hawks. But he'd stand in the wings like everybody else and walk like everybody else. The secret was something extra he had, which I suppose is acting, isn't it? When he'd go out on the stage, he knew how to do it.'

The tradition of acting is based on copying. It's passed on from one actor to another . . .

Tony Hopkins's acting is greatly influenced by Olivier. Vocally, mainly . . . I think all actors are. They hear, they copy things. They hear Olivier, and the same with Richardson or Scofield – they're just little tools to help you.

In the sixties, after being at the National for three years, Michael began to get restless and went to see Olivier one morning in his office to ask for better parts. Olivier answered, 'Certainly, Michael,' and he casually lifted the phone and nonchalantly flicked through the company register, asking, without a touch of irony: 'Now, who do you want me to fire?'

Michael was horrified and remained frozen to the spot, mouth agape.

'Derek Jacobi, maybe, or John Stride . . . Bob Stephens?'

Michael protested vehemently, 'No, no, no, don't do thaaaat!'

Olivier then said, 'Okay, well, then, no, I can't give them to you. If I were you, I'd leave.'

He then called Birmingham Rep and got him a job there, which Michael always said was incredibly generous of him.

4

'Get him away from me'

In 1964 Gambon was in Noël Coward's *Hay Fever*.

Coward wrote, 'I am thrilled and flattered and frankly a little flabbergasted that the National Theatre should have had the curious perceptiveness to choose a very early play of mine and to give it a cast that could play the Albanian telephone directory.'

Michael was in a bit of a sulk as he was Robert Stephens's understudy and wanted to be at the Royal Court, and he would arrive for work in a pair of dirty jeans and leather jacket, with a quiff. One day, Stephens was ill. Michael had to go on with an ear infection with black liquid oozing out, and Dame Edith Evans screamed, 'Get him away from me!'

On the last night, Michael subsequently reported that Coward had wished him 'Goodbye, sourpuss.'

Gambon made his film debut in Sir Laurence Olivier's *Othello* alongside Maggie Smith. He had first met Maggie as a spear carrier at the Old Vic and had almost been fired for being late for a rehearsal until he burst into the room in tears claiming that his mother had died that morning. Maggie had been incredibly sympathetic (though his mother subsequently appeared alive and well backstage).

Othello was based on the National Theatre production staged by John Dexter. One night, Maggie Smith as Desdemona came off stage. Michael had been standing upstage playing the Second Gentleman of Cyprus but had managed to gain the entire audience's attention. When questioned, he confessed a little coyly: 'Well, now I think of it, I might have been standing at an angle and gradually tilting to one side . . .'

Whatever he was doing, Maggie Smith became aware during an important speech that the attention was no longer on her, as it should have been, but on something happening behind her.

'After the play, she rushed at me,' said Michael, 'like a virago, a crazy woman, totally possessed.'

Michael enacted it all, wild-eyed in terror, and said that she then proceeded to pin him by the throat against a wall and said, 'Listen here, you little shit! If you ever dare upstage me again, I'll skin you alive and then throttle you. Do you understand?!'

Maggie always terrified him after that.

Aged twenty-seven, Michael played Othello. No more Second Gentleman of Cyprus: he was the lead. This being the sixties, white actors still regularly played black roles. Some BBC executive producers had come to see the production, to see Brian Cox, who was playing Iago, and six years Michael's junior, to secure him for an important role in a big series called *The Borderers*. Instead, after the show, they chose Michael. 'You can imagine that was extremely awkward. Poor Brian looked so depressed, and all I could say was "Sorry, mate."'

5

At full gallop

For Michael, *The Borderers* was a wonderful swashbuckling adventure and had twenty-six hour-long episodes, representing two years' hugely lucrative work. One series took seven months to shoot and another seven months the following year, which represented a lot of money. It was a historical drama series set during the sixteenth century and chronicled the lives of the Ker family and their rivals, the Armstrong clan.

The two clans frequently clashed over land, resources and power. Michael played Gavin Ker, the head of the family, a complex and pivotal character.

Michael was taught to ride by the Horse Guards and became an extremely proficient horseman. There was one scene he liked to recount where he had to ride at full gallop beside a loch which he had to do in one take.

It was completely nerve-racking, but he loved it, and purportedly he used to take his beautiful grey horse (Blackie) to the catering bus at lunchtime to feed him. They became great

friends, and Michael was very sad when they had to say goodbye at the end of the series.

His riding skills were also put to good use in *Sleepy Hollow*,
the film he made with Johnny Depp and a marvellous cast of
fantastic English actors who were all great friends, so the production was tremendous fun and Michael loved working with
the director, Tim Burton.

Michael's parents had visited him in Birmingham when he
performed as Othello and were shocked to be greeted by a
blacked-up Michael, covered in exotic jewels at the stage door, as
he had 'forgotten' to tell them what role he was playing.

One regret of Michael's was that as his father sadly died on the
opening night of *Macbeth* in 1968, he missed seeing his performance. His mother, he believed, always preferred his voice-overs
to his plays and thought his 'Mr Wisk', for an advertisement for
washing powder in which Michael was the voice of a washing
machine, was his crowning achievement.

He also said she thought seeing these adverts on television
was far more glamorous than going to Buckingham Palace to
receive his knighthood. Michael was always very grateful for his
flourishing voice-over career, which made him a fortune.

CHARLES DANCE

He would often talk about his mother, and the way he described
her evoked an image of a small, round-shouldered old woman
dressed all in black and with few teeth. One day he told me, 'I haven't seen Mother for a long time. The last time I saw her she said:

"Oh, Michael, Michael, it's lovely to see ya – what are you
doing now?"

"I'm at the Royal Shakespeare Company, Mum."

"Oh, that's wonderful! What are you doin' there?"

'I'm playing King John, Mother.'

"Oh, that's grand! But it must be awfully hot in that gorilla suit!"

"No, Mammie – not King Kong ..."'

The other times we worked together were during poetry or prose readings at Dublin's Gate Theatre. We were both part of a pool of people Michael Colgan would ring up to say, 'Come and read some Beckett or Pinter with us.' So, either I or perhaps Jeremy Irons, or Barry McGovern or Penelope Wilton, but always Gambon, would read to a packed house at that beautiful theatre.

I used to smoke in those days, and Mike and I would stand on the fire escape stairs at the back of the theatre and smoke endless Benson & Hedges. With a twinkle, Michael's storytelling skills came to life.

'My mother, a crane driver in Belfast, worked on the construction of the *Titanic*.'

His audience was always captivated: 'Incredible!' 'My goodness!'

Encouraged, he'd continue, weaving tales of her derring-do, single-handedly flying sorties and dogfights with the Hun for the RAF during the Second World War, deep into enemy territory. He had a medal of hers somewhere, he'd say, probably in a sideboard at home ...

In 1974, a breakthrough came for Michael when the actor-director Eric Thompson approached him and said very casually, 'Do you want to play this vet in these three plays?' He would go on to appear alongside Penelope Keith and others in Alan Ayckbourn's *The Norman Conquests*.

Tim the vet was an ideal vehicle for him: 'The vet in *The Norman Conquests*, who just walks through and daydreams a lot – I suppose that was quite close to me. I daydream a lot.'

He would say, 'The guy hasn't got a brain, he's an innocent, a fool', and observed that such characters were 'much more fun to play. *Man of the Moment* is one of those guys. And the vet in *The Norman Conquests*. He doesn't know what's going on. I find them very appealing.'

In 1990 Philip Oakes wrote that Ayckbourn should be awarded 'some sort of medal as the Actor's Friend ... Somewhere in the world, it has been estimated, the curtain is always rising on an Ayckbourn play.'

I believe that for Michael, laughter and tragedy were inseparable. He was so at home in the work of Alan Ayckbourn, which allowed him to navigate its complexities with remarkable ease. Often, he couldn't complete one of his favourite anecdotes because he was laughing so much that, like a child's, his eyes had filled up and tears were running down his cheeks. I remember an awestruck young actor once asking him what the secret of stage acting was.

Michael replied: 'You try to open the door, ignoring the sweat on your back. Then you try to step through the door. Then you try to close it. Then you get your first line out and you try not to look like a cunt. Then, if that works, you say your second. And you go on from there.'

Unsurprisingly, Michael was often Ayckbourn's first choice. This was something that always baffled him and he used to say mournfully, 'When I started, I thought of myself as a posh classical actor.'

True to form for so many classical actors, Michael could be superstitious. For example, he was extremely quick to remind me whenever it occurred that both he and Alan were a little superstitious about the word 'surprise', as, after all, it could equally apply to both a good and bad performance.

Famously, in one scene in *The Norman Conquests*, Michael, who although only six foot appeared much larger and had the ability to transform himself so that he became almost gorilla-like, was sitting at a dining table in a low chair.

Ayckbourn came in and sorted out the seating arrangements. In this respect he resembled Pinter, knowing immediately where the furniture should be so that everything fitted together like an intricate jigsaw. What they both admire is the calculated effect – one that can stun or excite or exhilarate a theatre audience. How they achieve it is down to their art and their brilliant timing and theatrical business.

'I feel entirely safe with him,' said Gambon of Ayckbourn.

'What he does, he does brilliantly,' said Ayckbourn of Gambon.

Their motto seemed to be: never look as though anything takes any effort and if you happen to be ignorant about anything, have the arrogance to think it doesn't matter.

'The play had a dream cast,' said Ayckbourn. 'There was Penelope Keith, Felicity Kendal and Tom Courtenay, but only Tom was a star in those days.'

Fittingly the biggest laugh – and one which established his reputation – went to the relatively unknown Gambon. Joining his fellow guests at dinner, he sank into the absurdly low seat, so low that only his head appeared over the cutlery.

'From that lowly seat began the rise to stardom,' wrote Eric Shorter in the *Daily Telegraph*.

Michael confessed, 'I deliberately made the chair even lower, so it was completely ridiculous seeing this man with the table coming up to his nose and having to lift his elbows right up in the air. Just the image of a man, quite a big man, sitting eating at a table with his arms up like that, eating a salad and then agonising over whether to drink a black or white coffee.'

The laughter, he said, 'came in waves and I thought it would never stop'. As he told an interviewer:

People couldn't stop laughing. They couldn't stop. The house shook. That was brilliant. Some nights all six of us would break. We hung on tight, but sometimes during that moment the laughter from the audience was so overwhelming you couldn't carry on with the play. So we would wait. It was like freeze frame. Penny Keith would stand there at one end of the table, and we would just wait until it got down. Then we'd punch in with the next line, and get on with it. I loved that moment. I remember one night at the Globe where we ran in the West End. I'm sitting in the low chair facing the audience. I was looking up and I saw a guy fall out of his seat in the back of the dress circle ... He was on an aisle, and he was laughing so much that he fell out of his seat and rolled down the gangway ... He fell out of his seat and rolled down the steps, and I thought, God Almighty, brilliant. Moments like that you never forget.

He told Philip Oakes: 'To call [Ayckbourn] a father figure is a lot to put on anybody, but acting is such a terrifying experience that I really do look on the director as a father.'

'Gambon is right about his willingness to take chances,' says Ayckbourn:

He's one of the most daring actors I know. If you are asking an actor to play a role, then as much of that actor as possible should get through to the part. A director can easily get in the way. I try to trot beside Michael like a sheepdog, pointing out a few gates he may like to inspect. [...] Michael does this superbly. He can adapt and improve and make something entirely his own.

Ayckbourn and Gambon had something else in common: they guarded their private lives fiercely. Michael and the mathematician Anne Miller married in 1962 and had a son, Fergus. Although he remained married to Anne, Gambon also had a second family with set designer Philippa Hart, whom he met on *Longitude* in 1998, and they had two sons, Tom, born in 2007, and William, born in 2009.

'But it's something I never discuss,' Michael would always say, although he proudly brought Tom and Will onto sets, and they always accompanied him to Tom Stoppard's bi-annual summer party at the Chelsea Physic Garden.

Michael said he wished he had kept in touch with Ayckbourn, though he confessed to his communication problem, being unable to write letters and terrible on the phone.

Alan Ayckbourn directed Arthur Miller's *A View from the Bridge* in 1987. Michael confessed, 'It was a frightening thing to do. I found it difficult to get on that stage, particularly in the opening of Act Two, when he comes in drunk. That's the scene where he kisses the boy. I found [it] very hard to psych myself up and get into the character of Eddie. Plus, the fact that you're playing a working-class man from New York. And it's about real people, not like Shakespeare. It's easier to step into the shoes of a king than to play someone who really lives and breathes and is modern.'

He remembered a question-and-answer session with Arthur Miller some time around then, in which they were asked if it was possible to be sympathetic towards Eddie. Michael said that he 'was relieved when Miller said yes, because he really doesn't know what he's doing; he's unaware of his own feelings about the girl' (Eddie's niece and Beatrice's daughter Catherine).

Part of Michael's enigma was his masterful ability to incorporate elements of play and lightness, even when portraying the most serious of characters and delighting the cast. It was a magical quality and cannot be stressed enough how Michael loved being playful.

Nonetheless, he always played comedy very straight, going directly to the essence of the character, and never played to the gallery. If it made him laugh, he felt confident. In more serious parts, he told me that he relied entirely on the 'little man in his head' to navigate him, which had been Ralph Richardson's treasured advice – that plus great direction.

Most of all he delighted in playing the role of the butler, waiters, or incidental, unassuming characters in the background of a scene and, through his superb ability at physical comedy, make them steal the show. Such as the total buffoon in the revival of *Tons of Money* or *The Butler* at the Aldwych. In some of his roles, such as in Beckett, he would stand at a perpetual tilt or lean against a door or another actor – as if each was about to give way. Traditional clowning, in a way.

Michael loved *Curb Your Enthusiasm* with Larry David, and he always wanted to appear in it in a short scene involving Larry and his agent Jeff having lunch in their usual restaurant. Jeff says to Larry, 'Look over there, it's the guy that played *The Singing Detective*,' and Larry would reply, 'WHO?' And they'd continue eating.

In fact, during one of our last conversations he repeated that what he wanted most was for someone to write him a play or film where he could play an intoxicated butler with no dialogue. It would go something like this:

A phone would be ringing in a room, and he would enter carrying a tray with an array of drinks – martinis, champagne, tumblers etc. – and try to find the phone without spilling the tray's contents. Of course, it would be hidden somewhere, and he would never succeed in reaching it before it stopped ringing or, if he did, it would be a wrong number. There would be very few, if any, lines, then he'd go bumbling out again. Always succeeding through incredible physical dexterity not to spill the drinks. Throughout the play, the phone would ring, and each time in would come the butler, maybe becoming increasingly sloshed.

6

'He wanted a banana'

Michael thrived on mischief and practical jokes. He adored them and his creativity knew no bounds. One such brilliant example happened on the last night of rehearsals of the Beckett play *Eh Joe* when he was performing at the Gate, Dublin, with his longtime friend, and hugely influential figure in his creative life, producer Michael Colgan.

Gambon's prank was a bit of fun between good friends. He purchased a card – a cheap, mass-produced one featuring kittens playing with yarn – and attached a review of the play. The *pièce de résistance* was a grainy, almost illegible image from the morning's paper, supposedly of Rammer Colgan, Michael's brother. The resemblance to Colgan was, at best, a bit of a stretch, relying on the shared features of a vaguely similar nose and the angle of the sun.

Underneath this photo Gambon had written in black pen: 'Rammer Colgan was pictured last night complaining to his brother Michael, artistic director of the Gate Theatre, about his latest production of Beckett's *Eh Joe*, which Rammer described as a "pile of shite". Rammer has been in Iran for the last 25 years, where he runs the National Theatre. He told the press yesterday that his brother's work was "a fucking disgrace".'

The card was pinned with the offending mock article in a prime position on his mirror, and Michael sat at his make-up table, innocently removing his eyeliner and waiting.

Knock at the door and in came Colgan.

There was always a delicious and playful banter between Gambon and Colgan, who spoke to each other like a pair of oul' Dubs straight out of a Seán O'Casey play.

'Are you having your dinner now?' asked Colgan.

'Can't you see I'm busy, doing this,' Michael gestured with his sponge and brush, with flustered irritation.

'Well, will you be coming over for a bowl of soup to the Gresham?' Colgan continued, oblivious.

'Yes,' snapped Gambon. 'But after I've done. Now get out!' He nonchalantly handed Colgan the card with the newspaper cutting, saying,

'This came for you.'

Colgan apparently then left the room without glancing at the card. Gambon loved this moment and always said, 'I'd wait and time him and precisely five seconds later. BOOM. Colgan's laugh would come booming down the hall. I'd have to come up with different things all the time. That was the kind of relationship we had, always jokin' about.'

Hiding in cupboards, in racks of clothes, putting on ridiculous hats and postures and voices were all part of this enormous playfulness.

A knock on the door and this tremendous "ELLO – what the fuck do you want?' before the door opened, timidly, followed by his: 'Forgive me, I'm an eejit, JUST MUCKING ABOUT.'

*

In 1975, Michael was cast in Edward Albee's *The Zoo Story* at Regent's Park Open Air Theatre.

Michael has often been described physically on stage as an animal – most frequently as a gorilla or a lion or bear.

'Is it the long arms and the rounded back, do you think?' he would ask pensively, then roar with laughter, gleefully swinging his arms backwards and forwards.'

Michael was particularly fascinated by the might and grace of the great apes. During the rehearsal period of *Zoo Story* he would walk across in his lunch hour from the Open Air Theatre to the zoo. He quickly became a regular guest of the keeper, and they would spend time in the room behind the enclosure. Guy the Gorilla first arrived at London Zoo on 5 November 1947. He was only a year old and spent the rest of his life in captivity there. Michael remembered seeing him as a child, when he used to climb through the fence into the zoo, and being utterly captivated by him.

This mighty creature was an incredibly gentle presence, adding to his fame and popularity, particularly with children who fed him large quantities of sweets, which he loved. (Sadly, it was his sweet tooth that led to his early death in 1978 from heart failure, while under anaesthetic during an operation for a tooth infection.)

Michael, spellbound, would study how Guy sat and the intensity of his gaze.

'Those wonderful ancient eyes, his untamed wildness and majesty. Gorillas examine things very closely.' (Michael would then pick up an object and demonstrate how closely they might examine things.) 'They pay huge attention to objects,' he would say, focusing on a lighter or his watch, carefully turning it over and scrutinising it in minute detail. 'They're constantly picking things up from the floor or inspecting their coat. Interested in everything around them.'

Michael used to say they reminded him of one of his heroes, the great Marlon Brando, who he worked with only once, in 1989, on *A Dry White Season*, the film based on André Brink's novel set in apartheid South Africa directed by Euzhan Palcy.

According to Michael, Brando had the same level of curiosity and intensity of observation.

Michael said one day the zookeeper asked him if he could keep an eye on the enclosure for half an hour while he popped out to run a quick errand. His only caveat being that under no circumstance was Michael to accept anything that Guy offered him. Michael was overjoyed to be given such an excellent opportunity to be alone with this tremendous creature. And, for a while, he sat entranced as Guy shifted his position, moved closer to the bars to study him, and stared deeply into Michael's eyes.

'I felt humbled to be locked in such an intimate moment with this majestic beast, his amber eyes filled with mystery and secrets, amazing power coupled with deep intelligence and sadness; he was deeply sad. Life imprisonment is awful! We humans, we are such fuckers.'

This moment was held unblinkingly until, very gently, Guy moved aside and shifted about his immediate vicinity. Then, slowly and deliberately, he revealed a long branch he had found on the ground. And with incredible precision, he began to feed it through the bars towards Michael who, overwhelmed by the magnitude of this gesture, had completely forgotten the keeper's warning. And, dutifully, he began to accept the branch, hand over hand, with incredible care, as though they were engaged in a form of holy communion. The ceremony lasted until this long stick, some six or seven feet in length and an inch in diameter,

successfully passed through the bars and was received by Michael.
Michael would mime this moment, his tongue stuck slightly out
in fierce concentration, slightly trembling in reverence.

Once the transaction had been successfully completed, they
sat and looked at each other. A BEAT. The gentle giant fixed
Michael with an air of expectancy. Not understanding the game's
rules, Michael began to feed the branch back with due solemnity
to Guy, who duly accepted his branch until it was fully returned,
when THWACK! He brought the branch down and smacked
Michael with a ferocious blow squarely on his head.

'OWWWW!' he shrieked, and in rushed the keeper … and
found Michael crouching in a foetal position with Guy towering
above him on the other side of the bars, flourishing the stick.

'Did you take the stick from 'im?' the keeper demanded.

Michael whimpered and nodded. The keeper shook his head.
"Ee didn't want the stick; he wanted a banana!'

7

'Oh, that's how it's done'

Ian McKellen noted that Michael had great luck with writers:

Gray, Hampton, Gill, Ayckbourn, Pinter, David Hare, Caryl Churchill, Poliakoff, all new writers, and of course Shakespeare. Also, he revered and loved Beckett from tragedy to comedy.

Even though our professional lives crossed working for Sir Laurence at the Vic and later with others on the South Bank, we never acted together. So I was just a long-distance admirer.

After his matchless solo of Beckett's *Krapp's Last Tape* at the Duchess Theatre (2010), I told Mike how often I was mistaken for him and wondered if the reverse ever happened. 'Good Lord, yes! They bring me their wretched 10x8s of Gandalf all the time.' 'And what do you say?' 'Nothing. I just sign your name: "Love, Ian".'

His powerful voice and presence served him in good stead in *The Life of Galileo* by Bertolt Brecht at the National Theatre in 1980, the first Brecht play to become a popular success.

David Hare said Michael's performance in *The Life of Galileo* was 'one of his two high watermarks ... The tender glutton and the intellectual were held in perfect balance, and he reached into the 1,200-seat Olivier as if it were his living room.'

To wide astonishment, Sir Peter Hall chose Michael above titans such as Colin Blakely and Albert Finney, who would have seemed the more obvious candidates. At that time, Michael had built his reputation on the work of Ayckbourn, Simon Gray and Harold Pinter. However, Hall strongly believed that Gambon was, despite contemporary opinion that he lacked the weight for the role, an actor with 'catastrophic power'. He asked John Dexter to direct, which became a transforming experience for Michael.

Michael's immediate reaction when Hall first asked him to play Galileo was astonishment, 'and I was, as usual, terrified. I didn't know the play. I had never seen it. I had read it. I was delighted and I just said yes.'

Michael was also frightened of John Dexter:

He had the reputation of being something of a tyrant, quite a formidable man. There was no mucking about, so you always worked to please him in case he shouted at you. But I quite like being pushed into the corner like John used to do. He would drive you through the play and make you work. And he's not really a tyrant, just a great director.

Dexter said: 'Despite a lack of intellectualism, he has a probing mind, the keenest powers of observation, and the integrity of an Old Master portraitist. He feels his way into a role and then takes an imaginative leap into another man's psyche.'

Michael arrived in a rehearsal room 'unencumbered by the

excess baggage of memories drawn from life. Instead, he has a sense of selective recall. Ideas and images "cook inside" him.'

Dexter went on to say, 'Until he has solved all the practical problems – how to move, how to speak, whether to turn on the right foot or the left – that volcano of poetry can't erupt.'

The *Sunday Times* called his performance 'a decisive step in the direction of great tragedy ... great acting', while fellow actors paid him the rare compliment of applauding him in his dressing room on the first night. Critics suggested that he even rivalled memories of the great Charles Laughton, who had created the role for Brecht.

Simon Callow says of *Galileo*:

[It] was a massive, very exposing challenge for Michael: four and a half hours of high seriousness, its hero broken by the Church of Rome but somehow surviving. Undaunted, Michael just got on with it, filled it, filled himself, somehow, with titanic power and fierce intellectual energy, but also tenderness and generosity. He never, to my knowledge, discussed the part, certainly not in rehearsal; he just did it ... I was playing Fulganzio, the little monk, who, about two hours into the play, addresses a lengthy speech to Galileo, begging him not to disturb the time-honoured order of the universe. Michael listened to this heartfelt plea with undivided attention, but out of the corner of my eye, I saw his long, tapering middle finger slowly, over the course of the seven-minute speech, extending, so that by the time I finished, it was fully erect. Not a single member of the audience would have noticed this slowly evolving obscene gesture; I, of course, did, and struggled quite hard to maintain the little monk's deep seriousness.

Michael acknowledged that the part 'tipped me into the heavyweight league'.

The critics agreed, proclaiming that a major classical actor had been discovered. Sir Ralph Richardson's nickname was now justified. He was indeed 'the Great Gambon', an accolade that stuck, although Gambon dismissed it as a circus slogan.

Michael admitted that after his enormous success in *Galileo* it took him a while to decide on what to do next, and eventually, after much dithering, he chose *Much Ado About Nothing* but couldn't connect with it. Adrian Noble observed that when Michael was at Stratford and watched Derek Jacobi play Benedick, he remarked. 'Oh, fuck, that's how it's done. That's how to bloody play it!'

He later confirmed that Derek Jacobi had opened a door for him. But he confessed that 'playing *Much Ado* was a downer, which in hindsight was good after having had such a tremendous success'.

8

Table manners. Or etiquette?

When it came to contemporary giants, apart from Beckett, Michael venerated Pinter, the man, the writer, the director, the actor. They had worked together in almost every combination: he had directed him, played opposite him and replaced him as an actor. Michael said: 'He never says things he doesn't mean. That's how he directs. Only do something if there is a reason – otherwise don't. I like that about him. No nonsense. Whenever I'm near him I go quiet, because he really knows what he's doing.'

In a tribute written after Pinter's death in 2008, Michael wrote:

Harold was very plain speaking, not going in for lavish phrases . . . He'd sit quite still on his chair, watching rehearsals proceed.

The thing to understand about Harold is that he just loved actors. He was an actor himself, of course. So he'd give you a lot of room to play around in your role, rather than being domineering or prescriptive as some directors might be. He liked flexibility and gave it to others.

Michael was reverential about the writing, describing Beckett's work as 'like a bible', and would never alter his lines. 'You couldn't add anything to Harold either, could you? It's too brilliant. It would be an appalling thing. When I go near him, I go quiet because I feel I'm in the presence of someone who really knows.'

Shortly after Pinter married Lady Antonia Fraser and was moving within ever-elevated social circles, he invited Michael to her house in Campden Hill, a very smart address in west London.

Michael was thrilled to be invited to dinner, only to find himself seated next to Harold, who painstakingly demonstrated the correct way to use cutlery.

'Bloody cheek,' said Michael, laughing, 'he'd only just been taught himself!'

Particularly piquant for two working-class boys rising to positions where they would be greeted by royalty and ambassadors and dine with aristocracy and heads of state.

Michael remained fascinated by the upper classes – their world a million miles away from his very different origins and upbringing in Camden Town – and he loved being invited to stay in grand houses surrounded by beautiful objects. He was also incredibly proud of his house near Gravesend in Kent, which he told me he had bought outright, with cash, from the Swedish ambassador.

'That's near to where Pocahontas is buried,' he would tell me with great authority. Then, putting on his poshest voice, he would add, 'There are the best examples of multiple styles of

English architecture demonstrated in one building anywhere in the country, from late seventeenth century to modern day.' He loved the fact that part of the house looked like a ship, and rumour has it that Nelson once lived there. It had nineteenth-century additions: a library, a huge art collection, and space for the cabinets containing his guns and watches. As for his clothes, he said that they were all immaculately hung and folded on racks and shelves displayed in a separate room.

Sometimes Michael would softly say, 'It's like a tribute to a man who doesn't know what to do with himself.'

Michael sometimes indulged in whimsical fantasies of simplifying his life. He'd picture himself in a small house somewhere on a street in South Kensington. The Ferrari, he'd declare, would have to go. 'It's not a London car.'

In 1978 came the first production of Pinter's *Betrayal*, a performance marked by subtlety. Michael is one of the few actors to have mastered the demands of the vast Olivier Theatre. As Simon Callow once said, 'Gambon's iron lungs and overwhelming charisma can command a sort of operatic full-throatedness which triumphs over hard walls and long distances.'

Many years later, Tom Hollander echoed that sentiment about Michael's wonderful power of delivery: 'That voice: that was a theatre actor's voice. We don't make them like that any more. Why? Because it is no longer normal to spend decades on stage in the way that generation did. Because people no longer smoke with that level of dedication. And because actors are now routinely microphoned in the theatre and so are not forced to develop that power.'

DAME PENELOPE WILTON

In 1978, Michael and I were in the first production of *Betrayal* at the National. The preview was nerve-racking, not only because we were opening a new play by Pinter but because the backstage crew were on strike, so we didn't know if it would actually happen. The country was going through a sort of nervous breakdown – as we are now.

The opening scene takes place in a bar where we have a couple of drinks.

Michael comes to our table with the first round: wine for me and a pint of beer for himself. But out of nerves, he put the beer in front of me and the wine in front of him. [...]

The first line is, 'Cheers!' Just before we said it he swapped the drinks, but then, rattled, he hit his teeth on the glass and all the beer went down his front. It could only go up from there. [...]

He was witty, entertaining and also extremely nice – a really sweet man in many ways. He could also be naughty.

Pinter said of Michael:

One of the things that he and I both share, having worked together so many times, is a concern about the physical state of affairs, where you actually are. If you are in the wrong place, or you can't find a way of getting to that place, you have to keep burrowing away. I feel as a director that I would like you the actor to get from there to there. The question is how you can justify it so that it's harmonious and true and coherent, where it isn't arbitrary.

And I think we work terribly easily together. We just look

at the thing itself and get on with it. His way of working is continually alive.

There's no question about it ... a great actor has come about. He really has just about everything – enormous power, great depth, absolute expertise and the ability to illuminate comically the character and the event by the simplest of means ... He goes for the heart of the matter and does it most economically and totally without sentimentality. He can arrest and compel. At the centre of this, he is a most delicate actor. I've worked with Olivier, Richardson, Gielgud, Scofield, Redgrave, Guinness and Peggy Ashcroft, the greats of English acting, and Michael Gambon is in that category.

Lady Antonia Fraser reminded me of one of Harold's favourite stories about Michael. This story has become legendary, and many actors love to retell it. It is concerning the actor Terence Rigby and his fear of flying. Apparently, it was holding this talented man back from accepting jobs in America, and so Michael decided to take matters into his own hands.

Michael said, 'I thought it was terrible. I took him up in a Cessna 180, which is a small four-seater plane. He was paralysed with fear and took a lot of persuading.'

And so Michael said, 'If you sit next to me in the right-hand seat, I'll do everything very gently, and you can see how a plane works.'

They took off from Biggin Hill. It was a gentle climb up. Then Michael levelled the plane out at around something like two thousand feet. Poor Terry was rigid with fear, white knuckles, sweating and hyperventilating, but after a while he managed to slightly acclimatise, calm down a little and breathe normally. At this point, Michael started to introduce him to the mechanics of the plane . . .

'If you do this, the nose drops; if you do this, the nose goes up, and this is air-traffic control I'm talking to.'

Then Michael said to him that they were going north to Essex, then to Ipswich for a cup of tea and a sandwich at a lovely little airfield. They flew over the Thames, and suddenly, from nowhere, the devil got into Michael – the same thing that makes him muck about in a play. He whopped a bit of rudder down, put the stick forward and took the plane into a very slow drop – and then he staged a heart attack. He did the whole thing – clutched his heart, cried out, gasped for air and collapsed against the side screen. Keeping one eye open to gauge the reaction of his passenger.

But to his amazement, Terence didn't do anything. He just sat there. After a moment, Gambon pulled himself together and apologised, saying it was only a bit of indigestion. Terence was furious but didn't collapse in fear. Neither did he ever speak to Michael again. He did, however, manage to fly to LA for work.

9

'He made a coin with two heads'

Alan Ayckbourn's *Sisterly Feelings* is famous for its choice of second scenes determined by the toss of a coin.

The coin toss is a complex and symbolic game that reflects the strained relationship between the two sisters, Abigail and Dorcas, in pursuit of Simon. Heads or tails: heads can be interpreted as Abigail's dominance and control, while tails represents Dorcas's vulnerability. Gambon notoriously favoured one scene over the other and, using the National Theatre's metalworking department, made himself a double-headed 50p to rig the coin toss. It was polished so no one could tell; the line was a fine one.

DAME PENELOPE WILTON

I played Abigail, and Michael was my husband, Patrick. Halfway through the play, someone tosses a coin, and that determines which sister's story is told in the second half: Dorcas's or Abigail's. Michael was a precision engineer before he was an actor, and he made a coin with two heads. I didn't know this, but most of the men in the company did, including the one who tossed the coin.

So every time, it was heads – which meant 'Abigail under Canvas', which meant my taking my clothes off in a tent with Michael, with all the boys getting to go to the bar in the interval, because they wouldn't have a costume change. I found out about the fix and so, the next night, I called tails. They weren't expecting that.

Michael made acting fun. That made him easy to work with, because he was so quick and instinctive. He was also very generous – when you were in a scene with Michael, he looked you in the eye.

On stage, his concentration was excellent. Off stage, it wasn't always so good. Yet he'd take direction extremely well if he admired the director – and not so well if he didn't.

Timing and a light touch are things you can't teach; you either have them or you don't. Michael had them. That's why he was wonderful in comedy but also why he was wonderful in Pinter, which requires you to be very deft, and in Beckett, who is also very funny.

He was aware of what he did to an audience and knew when he'd scored. On stage, he was a big man – yet he wasn't actually that tall. Nor was he the greatest looker of all time, but he had a sort of sex appeal. He created a lot out of very little. And for someone who was for a lot of his life quite large – he got much thinner as he got older – he was extremely light on his feet.

10

'Mike was a piece of limp lettuce,
and I was a feather duster'

According to Michael, the 1982 RSC season at Stratford had 'a very butch male company ... Pete Postlethwaite, Antony Sher, Malcolm Storry, a real heavyweight bunch of sweaty, effing bastards'. It was a pretty grim experience to be a woman in that company. However, one woman who held her own was Helen Mirren.

Adrian Noble was known for his rigorous and detailed approach, and often employed exercises that focused on physicality and vocal precision. He used improvisation where Michael and Helen played with status and power, exploring the shifting power dynamics between Antony and Cleopatra.

DAME HELEN MIRREN

In our first rehearsals for *Antony and Cleopatra*, our director, Adrian Noble, wanted to take us through improvisations to get

to know each other. At one point, Mike was a piece of limp lettuce, and I was a feather duster, and he was brilliant! He often
made me weep with laughter, and at the same time I could see
those incredible long fingers delicately remaking or mending a
priceless eighteenth-century musket. A man of contradiction.

In turn, Michael remembered those extraordinary rehearsals
with great affection and loved to recall and to re-enact them.

One of the exercises at Stratford with Adrian Noble: we
pretended to be animals. When we were doing *Antony and
Cleopatra*, it was just me and Helen Mirren in the big room. He
said, 'I want you, Helen, to be a rabbit and you, Michael, to be
a lion,' and he said [*snaps his fingers*], 'Now!' And so I became a
lion. I remember this was terribly funny, and he added quickly:
'There is a steel grille that has come down the centre of the rehearsal room, and there are bars running from me to the wall.'
So I went to the bars and looked at the rabbit: she was hopping.
I was padding up and down. I started off making a few noises [*a
low growl*], and she was going, 'Heh, heh, heh' [*panting*]. Rabbits
don't make a noise. After ten minutes of doing that, you get a
bit embarrassed. After about fifteen minutes the mind clicks
off, and you say, 'Oh, fuck this.' The bastard is sitting there
smoking, saying nothing and watching these two actors who by
that time are well out of character. So I went and curled up in a
corner and she curled up, and that was it. It must have been an
hour, and then in a loud voice, he said, 'The steel grille is now
being lifted up.' I thought, oh shit, and then he said, 'The steel
grille is gone, there is nothing between the two of you.' So I ran
over and killed the rabbit!

Michael said, 'We'd do *King Lear* in the afternoon, and then we'd nip to the Other Place and do *Antony and Cleopatra*. Having gone through that, you were really on the ball ... It's quite wonderful to play King Lear in the afternoon and then play Antony opposite Helen Mirren in the evening.'

Michael always said that performing with Antony Sher was a little bit like being in a boxing ring, that there was a healthy rivalry. But Michael was keenly aware that actors are selfish by nature – they have to be, to play leading roles – and by the time the play opened, he had begun to feel that the play as they'd rehearsed it was no longer King Lear's, because the Fool was so prominent.

Michael said, 'I imagine it's like playing a good game of tennis. The better the player you're opposite, the better you are. I'm being too simplistic, but a play, the meaning of a play, is the principle of the thing, not who's winning.'

As part of their rehearsals for *King Lear*, Antony Sher recalled that Michael practised the storm scene on Dover's Hill outside Chipping Campden with him 'roaring at jets passing from the nearby airbase'.

I still imagine the pilots looking down at a terrifying vision of Gambon embodying Lear's descent into madness and his confrontation with the forces of nature, a magnificent, deranged monarch shaking his fist and screaming up at them, 'Blow, winds, and crack your cheeks!'

Michael carried his lucky stone from Ralph Richardson in his pocket throughout his performances of *Lear*, because its solid touch grounded him. Richardson had told him to do this, both to help vocally and for ballast. Michael used to say, 'Call it superstition if you like. Some actors hang on to pennies. It gives you a feeling of solidity, that you're holding something real.'

Along with his stone, Michael had other more magical talismans. He wore an enormous ring on his little finger, like Sir John Gielgud or Paul Scofield. He said that he liked amulets as they connected him to the consanguinity of his acting tribe.

11

The year of Turtle Diary

Nineteen eighty-five was the year of a British film, *Turtle Diary*, directed by John Irvin with a screenplay adapted from the book by Harold Pinter, and starring Glenda Jackson and Ben Kingsley. The film is a quirky and gentle piece about two lonely individuals in London who are drawn together by a shared desire to free the sea turtles from their cramped enclosure at London Zoo. Michael liked Glenda Jackson immensely, though he couldn't understand why she needed to mess around with politics. And he loved working with Ben Kingsley as he constantly made him laugh.

It was a good year for Michael as he also appeared in the role of Dafydd ap Llewellyn in *A Chorus of Disapproval*, which won him the Olivier Award for Best Comedy Performance.

As David Jays wrote in a tribute after his death: 'Violence coursed through him, even in comedy: as the end-of-tether am-dram director in Ayckbourn's *A Chorus of Disapproval*, he raged at his amateur cast: ("I wish to God they were professionals. Then I could sack them.")'

*

Michael could very occasionally also be a monumental prima donna, as in one truly splendid dramatic meltdown while filming a BBC series about Oscar Wilde. *Oscar*, which first aired on in March 1985, was directed by Henry Herbert, the 17th Earl of Pembroke, who later became a great friend of Michael's.

He thoroughly researched the life of Oscar Wilde – 'Did you know,' he said to me, 'that Oscar Wilde had black teeth because of mercury poisoning?' (Mercury was then the only treatment for syphilis) – and tried to shove much of the research into his performance but became increasingly frustrated as the BBC objected: 'They said it was too much,' he would rage.

In response, he said to them, 'Too much?? Do you want the real truth about Oscar Wilde, or do you want some silly story? And do you know what those television people said?'

He put on his best Oxbridge voice:

'"Well, we can't have that on TV. You can't have black teeth."'

'So, I asked them, "Why are you making the story of Oscar Wilde?"'

'To which they replied, "Well, it's a good script."'

And Michael asked, 'But why are you doing it if you don't want it to be true?'

And they said, 'Well, the audience wouldn't like it, so sorry, Michael, no black teeth.'

Michael then, in the telling, looked deflated: 'It was weird and so that is why I got mad with those people.'

Not unsurprisingly Michael 'threw a moody' after a day of filming in Bristol. He returned to his hotel to change and prepare to travel to their next location in Oxford. It was 4 p.m. The day had gone poorly, and he was miserable. He arrived at reception resplendent in Edwardian costume, complete with a cravat, black wig, full make-up, and carrying a silver-topped cane, only to discover that his room had been double-booked, and his personal (civilian) clothes were missing. This was the last straw.

In a rage of volcanic proportions, Michael spun on his heel and ran out of the hotel, shouting obscenities. He dashed through Bristol with the production manager and a few assistant directors hot on his heels, Michael bellowing insults at them over his shoulder. It was an astonishing scene: Oscar Wilde, in full flight, careering wildly through the city centre, waving his cane threateningly while people darted for cover, and with the production team trying their best to catch him.

Michael then made a reckless move, dashing across a busy main road, causing chaos and near accidents as cars swerved to avoid him. His pursuers, guessing he was heading for the station, attempted a shortcut, but they were too late. They watched in disbelief as he vanished into the station, somehow managed to buy a first-class ticket and boarded a train to Paddington, still gesticulating and screaming profanities at them as it pulled away.

Once on the train heading for London, Michael went straight to the bar and got thoroughly drunk, and by the time the train pulled into Paddington he felt more mellow. Until, that is, he saw a group from the BBC waiting for him at the barrier.

Michael told me that all his anger returned, and, brandishing his cane, he threatened to harm them if they approached him. The bemused and terrified inspector accepted the ticket of the drunken and dangerous Oscar Wilde and allowed him to pass through the barrier.

Once through, he sped off, with the BBC in hot pursuit, racing through the station, foiling all their attempts, jumped into a taxi and escaped home.

As he recounted this story, he said, 'It was a terrible thing to do, but even though I knew I was in deep trouble, I couldn't stop; I regretted it but couldn't stop.'

The following day, at 5 a.m., his car arrived as usual and drove him to Oxford, where he was greeted as though nothing had happened. No one referred to the incident again. Instead, it was, 'Good morning, Mr Gambon. Would you like tea – three sugars – and a bacon sandwich?' His missing civilian clothes hung in the wardrobe, all beautifully ironed. His costume returned from his 'escape' across country, ready for shooting and immaculate.

'So, yeah', he would say, 'I can be temperamental. What did they expect?'

What Michael really wanted to do was play Oscar Wilde in Paris before he died. He said he had once read:

How Sarah Bernhardt, the famous French tragedian, saw him in the street. She recognised him as Oscar Wilde and invited him for supper. He turned up, and she expected him to entertain all her guests. Instead, he sat silently, ate his dinner, drank all the wine, and asked if she could let him have five thousand francs as he left. She said no. He walked out and died two months later.

'That's true, on my old mother's life,' he used to say. Even though, by this stage in our working life, his beloved mother was long dead.

12

'I thought you were the maintenance man!'

In 1986, Sir Peter Hall asked Alan Ayckbourn to become a company director at the National Theatre. To everyone's surprise, the first person Ayckbourn picked to join the company was Gambon, who immediately accepted. The entire community at the National was amazed by this news, as the plays had yet to be chosen at that stage. This was followed by his big break on television, the superb *The Singing Detective* by Dennis Potter, and he won his first Bafta for Best Actor.

This role would completely transform his level of celebrity; in America and England, it was a breakthrough piece of drama, a complete one-off and a fantastical film noir for television in which an invalided man lies in bed with a terrible condition called psoriatic arthropathy and fantasises about being Philip Marlowe, Raymond Chandler's fictional detective. He also leaves his hospital bed in dream sequences to become a dashing singer.

Michael admitted, 'It was complicated stuff. But I read it and I had to play it. I thought it was a masterpiece.'

Dennis Potter personally suffered from psoriatic arthropathy, whereby the knee joints, ankle joints, thighs, top of the spine and hands slowly fold in and get locked in that position, which was both agonising and debilitating. Michael said: 'I watched him holding a cup of tea and how he held a cigarette in rehearsals, little things.' He also said observing Potter provided him with something like 'a flow chart in your brain, a flow chart of emotions so that there is plenty of light and shade'.

On set, Michael was under tremendous stress, as he was required to lie in a hospital bed immobilised with extraordinary prosthetic make-up with terrible sores and lesions on his face. They had to shoot him first thing in the morning, otherwise the make-up started falling off. As Michael was unable to move his face, Potter noted, 'he used his eyes in amazing fashion'.

This experience on camera demanded a level of nuanced performance, of 'thinking big and acting small', that was invaluable for Michael's transition from the stage to the screen. He had to convey a vast range of emotions, often subtly through his facial expressions and minute physical movements. The close-up scrutiny of the camera lens – 'a lie detector at twenty-four frames per second', as Jean-Luc Godard famously remarked – required him to understand that, for the camera, less was always more.

After this series, Michael began to feel as relaxed in front of a lens as he felt in a theatre. Potter was another director who complimented him on his being very un-actorly and shy.

Michael put this very beautifully when he told me, 'Shy people look at the world more carefully, I think . . .'

Potter found it unnerving to be scrutinised by Michael in rehearsals – watching him very intently. 'I do remember at the read-through feeling vaguely unsettled by the fact that Gambon's eyes were never ever off, me sitting on the other side of the table and quite some feet away from him ... I think he was certainly noting my movements with my hands, with a perpetual cigarette ... I'm sure he wasn't imitating. He just registered it.'

Dennis Potter held him in extremely high regard. He hugely admired Michael's ability to navigate the character's multi-faceted nature – his cynicism, vulnerability, anger, bitterness and moments of unexpected tenderness. Potter often remarked on Michael's acting range and skill at inhabiting the complex character of Philip Marlow. His capacity to portray both the hard-boiled detective and the man suffering beneath the surface. To convey the character's inner turmoil and pain with remark-ably subtlety and power. For Potter, Michael was crucial to the series and the ideal actor to bring his vision to life:

There is a very fine line between parody, which is always boring and painful, and living within a parody and knowing it's a parody. It's just playing the role until you can start to relax and be whatever it is you are. That's very difficult to get to as an actor. There's something amazing about the ease in which Gambon can get to those places. If you looked at him walking along the street, you would say that his feet are slightly too heavy, that he had a couple of pounds of lead weight in them. That would be your first glimpse of him in your mind. Yet there's this nimbleness. The contrast between the immediate physical perception of him and what he can do is very wide indeed ...

You wouldn't be surprised to encounter him in a Dickens novel, as a kind of accountant's clerk or solicitor's clerk wear-ing patent leather shoes, who sits on a high stool like the other clerks – and does amazing things when he locks the office

door. There's something of that in him which comes out in
his acting.

Michael loved to sit in cafés with cab drivers, swapping stories
of their adventures, and was always delighted when he was mistaken for a cabbie. He prided himself on *not* looking like an actor;
in his mind he was more like a gunsmith or a bank manager,
maybe even a solicitor. However, he did like to wear a flamboyant
scarf on occasion which he thought was the equivalent of Bette
Davis having a small dog. These accessories were supposed to
mark them out as thespians.

He was cast in an episode of *Minder*, made at Twickenham
Studios, called 'Guess Who's Coming to Pinner?', in 1991. And
when he arrived at the studio, he couldn't find a parking space.
He'd arrived in an everyday work suit and overcoat and with a
big leather case and a rather brightly coloured scarf. A man who
seemed to oversee the car park came over and said, 'Not to worry',
that he'd take care of him 'from that day'.

Michael was naturally flattered, thinking it was one of the
perks of celebrity, and this went on for a couple of weeks until
the final day when the man came over to him. Michael put his
script on the roof of his car, and the man asked, 'What's that?'
When Michael told him it was the script they'd been doing.
The man said, 'Are you an actor? I thought you were the fucking
maintenance man!'

'Bloody cheek,' said Michael. 'I was wearing a flamboyant scarf
which is a dead giveaway for an actor, a bloody maintenance man
wouldn't be seen dead in a flamboyant scarf, would he?'

Michael also starred as the French detective inspector Jules
Maigret in an ITV adaptation of twelve of Georges Simenon's

books. The director, Nicholas Renton, also later directed Michael in a sensational production of Elizabeth Gaskell's *Wives and Daughters*, which won Michael a Bafta. The script was written by Andrew Davies and produced by Sue Birtwistle, with a stellar cast featuring Penelope Wilton, Bill Paterson, Tom Hollander, Justine Waddell and Keeley Hawes.

TOM HOLLANDER

I played Michael's estranged son once, in a BBC adaptation of *Wives and Daughters*. I died in a field. He had to carry my body back to the house, weeping. I was too heavy. For the wide shots I was replaced by a dummy. For the closer coverage, I lay on a sort of trolley, Michael bent next to it and put his arms under me and shuffled forward keening with grief.

They shot upwards. A blurry bit of me lolling. His arms, his chest, his face, the sky behind. Michael started giggling at the absurdity. Initially between the takes. Eventually during them. Still weeping. But also laughing openly. Weeping with laughter you might say. He got a Bafta for that one. [...]

People said he was careless with his gifts. Mostly directors and writers who found him difficult to control. But it wasn't true. Michael cared so deeply about his acting that when his powers started to leave him he hid it by playing the clown. The anxiety made him ill. But he covered it. There was a lot of cover with Michael. He was a complicated, unknowable man. And he was an artist. Though he would have scoffed at the idea.

He once told me he couldn't be bothered going on holidays because it was better to imagine them. He played his parts like that. He didn't research them. He imagined them. If you could imagine it well enough it was true. 'They've asked me to play a

twelfth-century German-speaking one-legged pope. You know
what? Turns out he's just like me.' 'I'm going to be playing a
Mongolian shepherd who dreams of being a trapeze artist. You
know what . . . ?' Et cetera.

13

Shaking hands with greatness

In 1987, Michael burst on stage, starring in Alan Ayckbourn's sensational revival of *A View from the Bridge* at the National. David Hare later remarked that Arthur Miller told him that Gambon was the best Eddie Carbone ever.

In the play, Michael performed an extraordinary balletic leap across the stage, and he confessed that, in another incarnation, 'I would have liked to be a ballet dancer.'

Michael was a brilliant shape-shifting actor and always imbued his performances with a physicality that belied his size. He used physical theatre a lot, clowning skills, slight caricatures. He possessed a remarkable ability to introduce physical comedy even into serious roles. He could, for example, use his large frame to create moments of unexpected clumsiness or exaggerated movements. He was the consummate master of the double take and the slow burn, using subtle facial expressions and body language to amplify comedic moments. His timing was impeccable. He wasn't afraid of being absurd or tilting towards the ridiculous, which of course, resulted in making his characters more human and relatable. He used his body to tell stories. A slouch, a swagger, a sudden dazzling burst of energy – these physical choices revealed character and advanced the narrative in ways that words alone couldn't. He often used physical comedy to expose the vulnerability of his characters. By allowing them to be awkward or clumsy, he made them more sympathetic and therefore accessible to the audience.

Getting the walk right was always mandatory for Michael: 'The walks just come with the learning of the character in rehearsal. They just seem to grow out of what the man's saying, and what his attitude is. Eddie Carbone is working on ships and lifting great heavy weights, so I thought that's the way he'd walk.'

DOMINIC WEST

I had been a fan since he played Oscar Wilde on TV, but it was his Eddie Carbone that made the greatest impression. I played the part myself this year [2024], inspired by his great performance. I remembered the way he modulated certain lines. He was fantastic. His towering bulk dancing on elegant, bench-made shoes. A massive presence capable of such vulnerability and raw humanity. And it was his humanity that made him such compelling company on and off stage. Behind every character, you sensed the melancholy.

He had a keen sense of the ridiculous. We were parents at the same school, and Michael was asked if he would mind talking to the kids about Dumbledore. To allay his panic, I was recruited to act as MC.

'The trouble is . . . I don't know a single thing about Dumblebore!' he shouted to me over the din of sixty expectant nine-year-olds, Dumbledore fanatics all.

'Neither do I!' I reassured him. There followed an excruciating grilling from five dozen world Dumbledore experts as Michael foundered like a dazzled deer, and I struggled to divert attention. It was one of the funniest twenty minutes of my life.

'Why did Dumbledore in Book 4 Volume 8 say the Jabberwock spell and not the Sinistrian spell when battling Obfuscitis?' Imagine Michael's look of pained helplessness. Hysterical tears welling in his eyes, moments from laughter. But the kids loved him. To them, of course, he was perfect.

In 1987, Elijah Moshinsky directed a terse interpretation of *Ghosts*, Ibsen's infamous and once scandalous story, for the BBC. Michael played Pastor Manders, who represents the rigid, moralistic and socially conservative values of nineteenth-century society. However, while preaching about duty and morality, Manders is often blind to the human cost of his rigid beliefs and lacks compassion. He's a prime example of the hypocrisy that Ibsen critiques in the play. The director used camera angles and lighting to create tension and drama that revealed secrets about the characters and their relationships. He also drew on nineteenth- and early twentieth-century painting traditions to build the atmosphere.

DAME JUDI DENCH

I think I've known Mike all my life. I can't remember when we first met, but I do remember that he and Ken Branagh and Freddie Jones and Natasha Richardson and I were all in a production of *Ghosts* directed by Elijah Moshinsky, and there was a very intense dinner scene after I had told Pastor Manders, played by Mike, that I had seen my husband, Captain Alving, kissing our maid, Johanna. Elijah just wanted to do huge close-ups of people. And he said, 'I don't want anybody speaking in it at all.'

Then he said, 'Action!'

And Natasha handed some potatoes to Mike, and he said: 'I'll just have the usual eight.'

Now, we just went to pieces, we completely went to pieces, and the next thing we heard was Elijah Moshinsky saying: 'Mr Branagh and Miss Dench, you may leave the studio.'

And we were sent out!

14

'Eight Uncle Vanyas *a week will break a man*'

Nineteen eighty-eight was the year of *Uncle Vanya* at the Vaudeville Theatre. Michael Billington felt that the production just failed to achieve greatness but wrote of Michael's performance:

> Michael Gambon has inherited Ralph Richardson's ability to exist in two dimensions at once. Half the time he seems to be living in a private dream: there is a magnificent moment when he is accused of being drunk and cries, 'Possibly, possibly' in a voice so alien and remote it might be coming from a man under hypnosis. Gambon offers a brilliant monument to ineffectuality: a man crippled by unrequited love and professional futility.

Harold Pinter marvelled at the fact that Michael was playing the sergeant in his play *Mountain Language* at the National, at the same time as he was doing *Uncle Vanya* in the Strand, and how he could somehow transform himself from one to the other in the short distance across the river. As soon as he had finished

Mountain Language a car would arrive at the stage door and scoot him to the Vaudeville.

Incredible though this sounds, Michael loved the challenge and used to say that he was, at his core, a champion of horizontal relaxation and fundamentally allergic to effort. But, terrified of this, he'd overcompensate by cramming his schedule with so much activity it could become surreal. A prime example: torturing himself by performing two plays a day.

By anybody's standards this was a prodigious achievement. But it also led to another instance of Michael behaving badly, this time during the six-month run of *Uncle Vanya*. In his defence, it was a Herculean task, added to the fact that Michael would become monumentally bored. In fact, he was, in his own words, 'going round the bend with boredom':

> Eight *Uncle Vanya*s a week will break a man. I snapped one Wednesday matinee. Twenty people in the audience, a near-empty house, and there, if you please, in the front row was a Picasso-wannabe cunt. He'd brought an easel, can you believe it? To paint Greta Scacchi. Fucking nerve! He wasn't even watching the play, and a red mist came over me. The cheek! Vanya's rage in the play, when he goes berserk – well, that was child's play compared to what descended.

Michael picked up the samovar. It must have had two gallons of water in it at least.

> I managed to take the lid off the top of it. I ran around the stage with the samovar – Vanya could do that – and at the right moment I engineered a trip . . . and I aimed the samovar at the man doing the painting. It hit him straight in the centre.

He was drenched. His oil painting was destroyed. Having done it, then you panic. This is going to be the end of my career. I'm going to be sacked. How could I do this? I turned my back and went upstage, trying to collect myself, to carry on with the scene. I turned around and he was gone. There was no evidence that he had ever been there. I thought, well he's waiting at the stage door, he's going to kill me. He's going to make me pay for all his clothes. It was terrible. The other actors were by that time not speaking to me. At the interval they were appalled, and I was just waiting to be beaten up. But he never showed up. And no one ever mentioned it.

It was well known that you needed to catch Michael early in a long run before he had a chance to get bored. The director Deborah Warner, who Gambon adored and flirted with relentlessly, recognised this:

He gets bored very quickly – isn't that the point? In film, I learned quite quickly that you have to film Michael's first rehearsal. I think he's the real acting creature. He's definitive and terribly terribly funny and very, very dangerous. But, in life, dangerous. His stories come out in many different forms. I'm not sure there is much line between reality and imagination, which is why he's marvellous.

Michael would always own up to this failing, then the mischief would arise. But he never repeated himself, and some of his alterations according to his word, accident or audience reaction might not be observable, but they were always there. This brilliance and ability to play two plays back-to-back only served later on to add to his melancholy as he described his fading memory being like a boat drifting further out to sea, leaving him. It was a monumental tragedy, and his fury and the loss at having to leave the stage, his world, his life and his deepest love, was incalculable. It called to mind a magnificent bull being wounded in the arena, and when he announced on the radio that he wouldn't be performing any more, I saw a part of him die. Much as Michael enjoyed film, it was on the stage that he reigned, and losing his ability to remember lines was a catastrophic loss.

I treasure what he used to tell me about the quintessential difference between the two disciplines: 'Acting is shouting in the night – film acting is whispering in the daytime. Stage acting is walking on a tightrope and film acting is walking on a white chalk line on the floor.'

Michael was obsessed and by American actors, and attributed his naturalism on stage and screen to the modern American school of acting – from the famous Actors Studio influenced by Sanford Meisner, Lee Strasberg and Stella Adler to such legends as Al Pacino, Robert De Niro, Dustin Hoffman and John Malkovich: 'That's who I would like to be. If I was born differently, with a different shape and look, I'd like to be . . . an American film star. I would! I think that's best of all.'

Ooh, Brando was wonderful. All he did was fuck about all day and tell jokes.

He pretended one day he didn't know what 'Action' meant. And the first assistant director was terrified of him, it was like meeting God! And he said, 'Um, oh, you have to start acting when I say that.'

And Brando said loftily, 'I haven't acted for about thirty years, and I don't intend to start now! Ha ha haaaah!'

But it was Brando who had led him into the profession and shone a light on his path. Brando he revered for 'his grace, intelligence, effortless ability to use the lens'.

He reserved similar adulation for Robert De Niro. Michael would say how he would walk barefoot across a stony desert to meet him. 'I think he's brilliant.' He often spoke of his work in *Raging Bull* as 'the most remarkable achievement, because there is not one frame of the film where he wants you to feel sorry for him'.

Michael, with his love of being a prankster, used to install a photo of the Hollywood star in his dressing room wherever he performed, signed: 'To Mike, best wishes and love forever. Bob.'

Of course, he wrote it himself, another of his inventions.

In 2006 De Niro directed him in *The Good Shepherd*, a spy thriller about the CIA's early years and one man's life within the agency. It is a work of fiction, loosely based on events in the life of James Jesus Angleton, named Edward Wilson in the film. Michael played Dr Fredericks, a Nazi sympathiser who tries to sexually seduce Wilson while at Yale and is later discovered to have been an undercover MI6 officer; eventually, he is murdered. Michael loved working on this film and often talked about the fun they had when they were in London:

I was walking down St Martin's Lane with Robert De Niro, on a busy Saturday night, and you walk as though you're his mate, you know. There were a few of us, and he said we were going to Sheekey's [a very smart fish restaurant]. I said, 'You won't get in there without booking.' Ha ha! To De Niro! He looked at me as though I was mad. A packed Saturday night, he walked in, and suddenly there was a big table, cleared!

He also said that De Niro and Al Pacino used to have mock fights whenever he met them in New York or LA. Michael would say something complimentary about Al Pacino to De Niro, who would respond fiercely, with something inflammatory and derogatory: 'What? That schmuck! That talentless M.F. Is he still being employed?'

Then he would say something similarly complimentary about De Niro to Al Pacino, who would respond with equal vehemence: 'That S.O.B. You dare to mention his name to me? How has he got the nerve to call himself an actor? That's what I'd like to know. I NEVER liked him.' And so it would build, this mock rivalry, until it reached epic, hysterical and tsunami proportions of abuse, Michael rigorously trying to defend the one to the other despite laughing at the outrageously exaggerated, preposterous and utterly obscene comments. One time, in LA, Michael was with De Niro, who told him that Pacino was filming downtown on a night shoot and that he could take him to the location so he could watch that – in De Niro's words – 'Completely talentless and worthless S.O.B. working, if that's what you'd call it – the lazy fuck!'

Naturally, Michael said he was very excited, so they set off late that night, around 11 p.m., in De Niro's car, for downtown LA. The film's location was Skid Row, where ambulances turfed out those without medical insurance – a scary, rundown part of town with bums huddled around fires in bins, shanty town tents, and dodgy dealers, prostitutes and derelicts hanging about with bottles in brown paper bags. A stench of desolation hung heavy in the air and from somewhere a jazz bar leaked music, smoky and slow with the sound of a double bassist who played like heartbreak.

For Michael, it was a scene of Hogarthian horror. Terrifying, lawless and bleak. After what seemed like an interminable descent into hell, they drew up at the entrance to an unsavoury rat-infested tunnel, at the far end of which could be glimpsed the big arc lights of a film shoot. It was a sinister and altogether daunting prospect. The car door opened, and Michael was pointed in the direction of the shoot which he approached with extreme trepidation, looking back several times at De Niro, who was smiling broadly from the car and waving him cheerfully on.

Michael said he got halfway down and saw something moving that could have been someone lying in wait to mug or kill him. A torch was shone in his face, terrifying him. So he legged it back to the car. De Niro, feigning surprise, said he thought he would have wanted to stay longer. Michael said breathlessly, frightened out of his wits, that he thought Pacino wasn't in that scene and that an assistant director had sent him back.

The next day, Pacino and De Niro were roaring with laughter about setting Michael up: Pacino was in his trailer and had been on the phone to De Niro throughout. The mysterious figure had been a runner waiting to take him on set and had been surprised to see the great man turn tail and run before he could get close enough to identify himself. Michael laughed about it but felt he had failed the bravura test of these two titans.

His experience with Dustin Hoffman was gentler, and Michael fondly remarked that 'when I saw one of his plays, he would say, "What didn't you like about my performance?"' He always felt flattered that Dustin respected his opinion.

Later, Michael was in his film *Quartet* and gave a wild and excellent rollercoaster performance as Cedric Livingstone, a pompous character who organises a fundraiser for the retirement home where the protagonists, four elderly opera singers, all live. *Quartet* marked Dustin Hoffman's directorial debut and was reportedly huge fun. None of them took themselves at all seriously – least of all Michael, who had riotous fun improvising most of his lines.

15

*'When you have to choose
between the truth and the legend,
choose the legend'*

J ack Lemmon met Michael in 1989, preparing for
Veterans Day.
'Who the hell are you, and where's Harold? I've flown across
the Atlantic to do this play, and is this a joke? Where's Harold?
I demand to see Harold.'

The lead-up to this infamous encounter was that Michael had
been rung up by Harold Pinter who said, 'I'm just about to play
this part and I can't do it. Will you do it?'

And Michael, realising that it was a four-month slot, flicked
through the script. There were two people in the play and
the other actor was going to be Jack Lemmon and so Michael
thought this was wonderful.

Lemmon plays a gung-ho used-car salesman and Second
World War veteran who uncovers a presidential assassination
plot in the local veterans' hospital. Involved are a Vietnam War

hero (Michael Gambon) and a mute Second World War veteran in a wheelchair (Robert Flemyng).

Flicking through, Michael saw there were long monologues for his character about injustice and that it was dramatic, and he thought this was fabulous, said yes and didn't bother to read the play. Then came the read-through where they got to stand up together in the rehearsal room, and Michael realised that the play just didn't work. After the read-through Michael said, in spite of his being so excited to work with this amazing co-star, 'Mr Lemmon, this play is a pile of crap.'

And Jack Lemmon said, 'How dare you say that to me. I've come all the way from Los Angeles with my wife. We're staying at the Dorchester Hotel. I don't know who the fuck you are. I'm American, I'm optimistic. What are you doing the play for?'

Michael said that he apologised but didn't change his mind. It really wasn't a happy experience even though working with Jack Lemmon was delightful. But he added that on the first night, as they were standing in the wings, ready to go on, Jack Lemmon turned to him and said, 'Michael, this play *is* a pile of crap.'

And he was right; it was a mess. In the end they went to the management together and 'begged them to take it off, as it was utterly unbearable – good fun being with him but night after night, God Almighty – and thankfully they did'.

The critics hated it.

16

'Without one redeeming bone in his body'

In 1989, Gambon starred in Peter Greenaway's crime drama *The Cook, The Thief, His Wife & Her Lover*, which also starred Alan Howard, Helen Mirren, Tim Roth and Ciarán Hinds. Gambon played Albert Spica, the thief of the title, a violent gangster.

The film premiered at the 1989 Toronto International Film Festival. Before filming started, Michael visited Olivier in Sussex at his cottage to pay his last respects to the great man, as he was dying. His wife, Joan Plowright, opened the door and whispered to Michael that he could briefly see Larry, but that he was not to excite or upset him under any circumstances.

Michael agreed and entered the room, where a significantly diminished Sir Laurence lay on his bed. He beckoned Michael over to sit close by him and asked what he had been doing. Michael said he had been offered a film by a director called Peter Greenaway.

'Oh, really, is it any good? What's it about?'

'Well, it's a kind of modern-day revenge tragedy with this horrible bastard, Albert Spica, without one redeeming bone in his body. He is a gangster, a thug, and he buys a posh restaurant where he terrifies the clientele. He tips a tureen of soup over a diner's head. He knees a bloke in the bollocks while he's having a pee. He runs this gang of murderers who create havoc, and he is married to a posh bird, Georgina – Helen [Mirren] will be playing it – and she has an affair with a bloke who is refined and likes reading. Alan [Howard] is playing him – a "bookish man".

'They start having an affair and have it off in the pantry. He finds out, goes berserk and smashes the place up, demanding that they hand him over.

'Eventually, he finds out where he is hiding, in a secret library. Spica smashes his way into the place, tears it apart and rips books off the shelves, tearing out pages and holding his victim down, forcing him to swallow pages of these books. He stuffs him full of paper, which causes him to suffocate and die horribly.'

Michael said that, by now, Olivier was no longer lying prone but sitting bolt upright, agog, saying,

'AND ... AND, THEN WHAT HAPPENS??'

'Well, and you won't get over-excited?'

'I will NOT get over-excited,' he said, trembling with anticipation.

'Next, Georgina persuades the French chef at the restaurant to cook her dead lover and invites Albert to a ceremony at the restaurant where she serves him to Albert, who has to eat him at gunpoint.'

At this point in the story, Olivier tried to throw his bedclothes off, bellowing at the top of his voice:

'Call my fucking agent! This is MY PART! This is the part I've been waiting for! FORGET IT – I'LL PLAY IT!'

Soon after, the great man died.

*

When Michael first received the script, he thought it was 'side-splittingly funny'.

It was an extraordinary production. Michael shared some of his process with us. Shoes were of vital importance to him; they grounded him. He stole pairs from production and filed the heel down on one side to help him develop a limp with his swagger.

He liked formal English toe-capped shoes of the kind a butler would wear. He then wore them playing smart people and ordinary people to see how it changed the performance. Comedy and tragedy sometimes performed in the same shoes.

As the thief, as part of his preparation he decided that he had been shot and knew the calibre of the gun because he knew what the Krays used to carry in the sixties.

Next, he had a list of names in his wallet of the money owed to him and by whom, and who was the next to be visited by his sinister lieutenant, a terrifying Tim Roth.

Alan Howard, who played the lover, was someone Michael knew and hugely respected and admired. At the RSC, Michael and Alan were both involved with Helen in the sixties, and she had bought them both little gifts during their separate liaisons.

All these years later, the three of them were cast in *The Cook, The Thief, His Wife & Her Lover*, and it was highly amusing for the wardrobe department to see that, in a very understated competition, each man would arrive in the morning wearing either a tie or sporting a pair of cufflinks, a lighter or even, I think, carrying a cigarette case that had been bought them by Helen, and the other, instantly recognising it, would casually remark, 'Oh, I say, that's nice, I've got one quite similar to that', to which the other would say: 'Really? Oh yes, a very dear friend gave that to me as a token of her affection.'

Helen remained aloof. From the moment she told Greenaway

that, as a vegetarian, she wouldn't be able to perform a love scene in a butcher's truck with the carcasses of slaughtered cows and pigs swinging from S hooks, she knew it was going to be an extremely challenging production.

In February 1989, in the stark setting of Elstree Studios, a sense of foreboding hung heavy in the early morning air, mixing with the mingled scents of bacon, cigarettes, coffee and sweat. The clattering of equipment, the crackle of walkie-talkies and the heating system's soft hum all added to the backdrop of the first day's shooting. Already in the make-up bus, the enigmatic and elegant Ms Mirren sat in stoic silence, her face a blank canvas awaiting transformation. Ciarán Hinds, Ron Cook, Ewan Stewart, Gary Olsen, Tim Roth and Roger Lloyd Pack exchanged banter in the communal dressing room.

At the stroke of six, a thunderous cacophony shattered the uneasy calm. A BMW burst through the gates at top speed, tyres squealing, rubber burning, and, as it started lapping the studio car park, came the howling of a banshee unleashed from hell demanding: 'Where's me boys?'

Albert Spica, embodied by the formidable Michael Gambon, jet-black hair slicked back, with the twisted yet swaggering gait of a gunslinger at high noon, had arrived, and, baying at the top of his voice, entered the building.

His menacing presence sent seismic ripples of fear and electric excitement through the cast and crew. Instantly, he transformed his gang from urbane and charming men into a feral pack of terrifying villains and monstrous thugs.

17

He accidently pirouetted backwards off the stage

Michael was once having dinner with Kenneth MacMillan when he was director of the Royal Ballet. According to Michael, he had seen him in a play, *Tales from Hollywood*, and wanted to cast him as Friar Laurence in *Romeo and Juliet*.

Well, of course, Michael was beside himself with excitement. Tragically, two weeks later, Sir Kenneth died from a heart attack backstage at the Royal Opera House and Michael was 'robbed' of his opportunity. He said, 'Kenneth felt I had "a dancer's heart" and not only did I believe him, I agreed.'

He later told Geraldine Bedell, in an interview for the *Observer*, that he had once been employed by the Royal Ballet, but he accidentally pirouetted backwards off the stage, landed in the orchestra pit, and broke the timpani.

One of his favourite memories was going to see Baryshnikov and Lynn Seymour in Prokofiev's *Romeo and Juliet*: 'Jesus, that's the greatest theatrical experience I've ever had. In the famous music, where the whole court comes down, I was in the second row. I found it just overwhelming. But I always felt that about ballet.'

18

'I'm not saying you're wrong, I'm saying you're naive'

In 1995, Gambon starred in David Hare's *Skylight* with Lia Williams, which opened to rave reviews at the National Theatre. The play transferred first to the Wyndham's and then to Broadway for a four-month run, which left him in a state of advanced exhaustion.

'*Skylight* was ten times as hard to play as anything I've ever done,' he told Michael Owen in the *Evening Standard*. 'I had a great time in New York, but wanted to return.'

He also alluded to potential tensions within the company, suggesting that there had been arguments between the actors, and Michael didn't finish the performance feeling happy. Nonetheless, he was nominated for a Tony Award and his performance was described as 'a masterclass in acting', praising his technical skill, his emotional range and his ability to fully inhabit the role of Tom Sergeant.

Michael also felt flattered that David Hare may have written the character specifically with him in mind because he refers to the character's big hands.

DAVID HARE

He was a great actor without any of the nonsense that sometimes goes with it. He could have breezed through *Question Time*, but he preferred to do *Top Gear*.

By the time Michael Gambon appeared as Tom Sergeant in my play *Skylight* in 1995, he was already having difficulty learning lines. It wasn't for lack of effort. Every morning he drove in with the script on the wheel of his car. After Princess Margaret came to see the play, she said rather sourly that it was a very good play, but that I was overly fond of the F-word. I didn't like to explain to her that most of the Fs were improvised. Michael simply used that same familiar word over and over, vamping to give himself time to think what the next line might possibly be.

Once the text came more easily, Michael liked to show off his mastery by inserting swathes of *Skylight* into performances of *Volpone*, which he was giving in repertory at the National Theatre. He remarked to a fellow actor that nobody understood a word of Ben Jonson anyway, and that if he chucked in some Hare, people would be none the wiser.

Michael took *Skylight* into the West End in Richard Eyre's production, and then we all went to Broadway, always with Lia Williams playing opposite. But despite huge financial offers, Michael refused to extend. He was slightly superstitious about success, always wanting to move on and do something else.

———————————

Bill Nighy took on the mantle of Tom Sergeant and went on tour with *Skylight* in 1997, then performed the play again in the West End in 2014. As he recounted in an interview on *This Cultural*

Life for the BBC, playing the part so indelibly etched by Michael was no small feat. Michael had wanted Bill to be his successor in this role, and encouraged David Hare to consider him.

Bill Nighy had always greatly admired Michael and once even sent him fan mail, to which Michael responded by thanking him for his support and saying he was wearing it! The effortless ease in which Michael inhabited the stage was for Bill a kind of holy grail of performance. Even the teasing he received from Michael once he started working at the National kept his spirits buoyed up: being called a 'bastard' in the canteen queue for example kept him feeling valued and supported for months.

Matthew Warchus had already established himself as a major force in British theatre who was not afraid to take risks and push boundaries, making him a fascinating figure to direct *Volpone*, Ben Jonson's satirical masterpiece.

MATTHEW WARCHUS

I was a very wet-behind-the-ears twenty-nine-year-old when I walked into the huge rehearsal room at the National Theatre to direct *Volpone* with Michael Gambon and Simon Russell Beale in the lead roles. It turned out to be one of the most joyful experiences of my life. Michael was not only the iconic barnstormer I'd seen melting the TV screen in Dennis Potter's mind-blowing *The Singing Detective* or giving a performance for the ages as Eddie Carbone in *A View from the Bridge*, he was also one of the funniest and most mischievous people you could ever hope to meet. I spent a large proportion of our rehearsal time hooting with laughter. [...]

The role of Volpone was a kind of playground for him: a

crook in his vigorous prime who feigns imminent death from a mysterious terminal illness in order to leverage gifts and donations from various sympathetic and wealthy visitors. To see Michael instantly transform himself, at the sound of a footstep in the hall, from bounding around with energetic glee to shrunken and quivering, tucked up in bed, was just endlessly hilarious.

Whatever he was in, he was a riveting actor to watch, and often did both power and feebleness in the most vivid and extraordinary way. He was undoubtedly a great physical clown – shades of Tommy Cooper – with mesmerising long-fingered hands and a body he loved to contort in unpredictable spasms of voltage. His voice, too, had so much impact, being somehow three-dimensional with an orchestral range of variation from sonorously booming to the daintiest fluting plus everything in between.

SIMON RUSSELL BEALE

Because Mosca [in *Volpone*] does all the work, I think Michael [as Volpone] saw himself as coming on and doing the odd big number, the seduction of Celia, or the mountebank scene. I think it was cleverer than I realised at the time because I was quite puritan about how you do plays.

The relationship between the two [Volpone and Mosca] is very, very funny. I loved working with him, and I think he loved working with me. And we're completely different, not in theatrical backgrounds, but in attitude.

I think he takes acting deeply seriously. But I think he had an idea of joy on stage that was above and beyond the text. He knew the play could survive if those two central characters were having as much fun as Simon and Michael were – which I hadn't realised. That was the difference between us, but, as I say, there are more similarities than differences in the sense that he's 'RSC', as I was.

––––––––––––

Michael was a demon in the play by making the other actors corpse – and he said with huge pride:

> I used to break everyone up, especially one scene in *Volpone* where the manager has just arrived in town and speaks Latin and gives a long speech to the townspeople which nobody under-stands – it's all bollocks – so I didn't bother with that. Instead I had an Italian accent and brought in all my favourite American movie stars in there, all sorts of stuff. Frank Sinatra – I used to sing 'I did it my way' in this Italian accent. I like to think it enriched Jonson's *Volpone*. You could see the audience going, 'What?' I thought it was legitimate, and Matthew, the director, didn't seem to mind. It made the scene funny, and I think Simon would agree. *Volpone* becomes more difficult as the play goes on as at the end he is unmasked as the old fox he is, and it becomes serious.

Michael really liked Simon Russell Beale and greatly re-spected him, even though they were from different generations. In fact, that was a tremendous help because, as Michael con-fessed to me, had they been contemporaries, he might not have been so generous.

He said that he kept a keen eye on Simon, following him with 'eyes wide open' as he was conscious he was snapping at his heels in terms of getting parts. He added wryly, after he heard that Simon wanted to play Galileo and was considering Falstaff, 'maybe by the time he completely erases the memory of *me*, I'll be too old to worry about it'.

19

'What an absolutely wonderful moment'

With the RSC in 1996, Michael starred in Yasmina Reza's two-hander *The Unexpected Man* with Eileen Atkins, first at The Pit in the Barbican and then at the Duchess Theatre, where he spoke these inimitable lines: 'Did I write what I wanted to write? No, never. I wrote what I was capable of writing, not what I wanted to,' says his character Paul.

'All you ever do is what you're capable of.'

DAME EILEEN ATKINS

One afternoon we were told that Princess Margaret was coming to the play with a companion and we were asked if we would stay after the show and be presented. Michael made one hell of a fuss. 'What the fuck for? I don't give a shit what she thinks. I'm not going to hang around to do all that rubbish.'

I said, 'Oh, come on, Michael, it won't hurt you. Just a few minutes for someone to tell you how wonderful you are.' Grumbling, he agreed to go. So, after the performance we went.

She had Ros Chatto [the famous theatrical agent] with her, and they seemed to have liked it. And then the conversation came to a halt. Nobody was saying anything.

I know that you're not supposed to ask questions, but I felt I had to. So, speaking quite truthfully, I said, 'You know, Ma'am, we're really glad you genuinely seem to love the theatre. Tell us what you have seen lately that you've enjoyed.'

Her face lit up at once.

'Oh, *Oklahoma!* – I'd seen it once and simply had to take Mummy for a birthday treat – and you know at the end the whole company, on the stage, sang "Happy Birthday" to her.'

Before I could say anything, Michael said in the most cringing tone: 'Oh, Ma'am, what an absolutely wonderful moment that must have been. The whole company singing for your mother – it must have been a great memory, one she never forgot.'

The thought that the cast of *Oklahoma!* singing 'Happy Birthday' to the Queen Mother should be a great memory was just ludicrous and I began to giggle, after which I could hardly stop. As soon as we got outside the door Michael said, 'Was I a cunt?'

20

'Steak and chips with no Russian sauce'

Michael Caine and Michael Gambon appeared together in two films set in Russia, both part of the Harry Palmer thriller franchise: *Bullet to Beijing* and *Midnight in St. Petersburg*. Later, they would appear in *The Actors* and the Hatton Garden heist movie *King of Thieves*. They had been long-term friends since the Buckstone Club days.

Michael loved telling the story of how he and Michael Caine had visited a Russian restaurant in Moscow while they were filming. It was a regular haunt of Caine's and he got on well with the maître d'. They settled in and the waiter came to the table, smiling, and asked what they fancied. Without glancing at the menu, Michael Caine said, 'I'll have my usual,' and Michael G said, 'I'll have what he's having,' so the waiter replied, 'Certainly: two steak and chips with no fucking Russian sauce.'

In *Midnight in St. Petersburg* Michael played a Russian interrogator and had to speak with a Russian accent. Between takes, he asked Michael Caine what he thought of his Russian accent and was told: 'Very good! It started off in Russia, drifted over towards Spain, was in Italy at one point, entered France and ended up in Lewisham.'

The Gambler (1997) starred Michael as Fyodor Dostoevsky, struggling to overcome his gambling addiction while writing his famous novella of the same name. It was filmed primarily in Budapest, which served as a stand-in for nineteenth-century Russia and Germany.

Karin Van Der Werff and Constance de Vos, in the film's art department, knew Michael well from having worked on *The Cook, The Thief, His Wife & Her Lover*, and Karin recalls some classic Gambon scenarios. They were shooting in Sopron on the Austrian–Hungarian border. Michael had the day off and spent it watching a Hungarian mechanic work on a car's engine. Neither could speak the other's language, so they communicated by humming and sharing his pack of Benson & Hedges.

On another day off, they came upon Michael sitting on the pavement outside a watchmaker's shop in Budapest, watching them work and showing his prowess at repairing watches.

At some point during the day, Karin and Constance started talking to Michael about a second-hand watch Karin had bought. In Hungary in those days, there were shops that were overseen and sanctioned by the government, to which citizens could bring their valuable items and sell them. Of course, the shop probably took a high commission, and the rest went to the owner; this meant the prices were regulated and controlled and for wealthy tourists from the West remained reasonably priced.

Michael said, 'Show me – let me see it.'

Karin said, 'Well, I was slightly nervous, as we knew he was very interested in watches and something of an expert. I hoped that I hadn't been sold a dud, as he really knew the difference.'

Anyhow, he looked at it, examined it minutely and eventually looked up with a smile and said: 'That is a beautiful watch and for a fair price – want to sell it?'

21

Her Majesty's adviser

Throughout the 1990s Michael moved seamlessly between stage, television and film, showcasing his remarkable range and versatility. Two distinct directorial visions also emerged with impactful films, both released in 1999. Michael Mann's *The Insider* was a gripping thriller exploring corporate malfeasance and the personal cost of whistleblowing, beautifully realised with Mann's signature style of intense almost hyper realism and meticulous detail. In contrast, Tim Burton's *Sleepy Hollow* was a superb gothic horror fantasy that drew its inspiration from Washington Irving's classic tale and brilliantly succeeded in solidifying Burton's imaginative and darkly whimsical storytelling with his delight in macabre and fantastical worlds. It was a period of complex narratives and stylistic innovation, and Michael relished the opportunity of straddling both genres and creating nuanced and memorable characters.

MICHAEL MANN

I knew I needed an actor with a presence that was sinister, ironic and dangerous but also so dimensional and dynamic you couldn't perceive his outer limits. That was because the character has only one scene in which to personify Big Tobacco, the hostile force against which all else conflicts for the length and scale of the two-hour forty-five-minute picture. Michael's performance is so riven with irony, threat, Middle American contempt and malice-as-sport that it radiates throughout.

He became the face of unbridled corporate capitalism's ability to destroy Wigand's life. How Michael's Sandefur moves his fingers, luxuriates in parodies and mock flattery, his posture is, for me, a masterclass in acting in three and a half minutes.

Gambon was absolutely a joy to be around, albeit dangerous, because you could sit for a quick dinner and four hours and three bottles of wine later, you were still there, four hours away from an early call. [...]

We worked together again on HBO's *Luck*, along with Dustin Hoffman and my late friend Dennis Farina. Artistically, Michael had no fear. He populated a character and moment with total focus, intelligence, and that unique quality of his.

———————————

Sleepy Hollow was filmed in 1998 in the grounds of a stately home near Windsor. Michael and Johnny Depp were having a break one day when the Queen rode past with her friend Henry Herbert, the 17th Earl of Pembroke, who had worked with Michael on the *Oscar* television series.

According to Michael's version:

As they went past, I'm standing there with Johnny Depp and some of the actors, having a fag, and a cuppa and Henry shouts, 'Hello Mike!'

So I reply: 'Hello, Henry, how are you, mate?'

The Queen then waved in our general direction and Johnny Depp says, 'Do you know the Queen then?'

I replied, 'Oh, yeah, we're mates, I'm always nipping in for tea with her every Thursday to discuss state matters – you know, to help her.' [*Tapping nose conspiratorially.*]

Johnny D's mouth was agape.

From then onwards he was convinced that I was some kind of very important adviser like spymaster Sir Francis Walsingham was to Elizabeth I.

Once the filming of *Sleepy Hollow* was finished, if Michael was ever irritated that a director who he hadn't worked with wanted to meet him – he felt they should have known his body of work by then – he would tell his then agent, Harriet Robinson, to send them the model of his decapitated head from the film.

22

It scared the bejabbers out of him

*The great Gambon is back on the West End
stage, and all is well with the world.*

Daily Mail

Cressida by Nicholas Wright premiered at the Albery
Theatre in London in 2000, directed by Nicholas Hytner
and starring Michael Gambon as John Shank. The company consisted of Charlie Kay, Anthony Calf, Michael Legge, Malcolm
Sinclair, Matthew Hickey and the young Lee Ingleby.

A comedy-drama, *Cressida* plunges into the seedy yet dazzling
world of seventeenth-century London theatre under Charles I.
Michael embodies John Shank, an actor and talent scout, who
finds himself on the verge of destitution having borrowed a
large sum of money to open a theatre company which has gone
under. His only hope rests with Stephen Hammerton (played

by Michael Legge), a naive fourteen-year-old who has been aban-
doned by both his parents and a previous master. Shank takes
on the task of training this new boy in the hope of transforming
him into a brilliant actor and then selling him for a huge profit.
Ironically, Stephen achieves immediate success when he aban-
dons Shank's tutelage and offers his own feminine interpretation
in *Troilus and Cressida*. As a consequence of this deviation from
his training, Shank, feeling betrayed, falls ill and his emotional
turmoil grows and causes his death.

In his programme notes, Wright reveals that most of the
characters depicted in the play really existed, with details gleaned
from letters and other sources.

Michael said that this was one of his happiest plays and he
adored the company.

The critics thought Michael's performance was a masterclass.
Darren Dalglish of London Theatre wrote: 'His resounding clear
voice is a dream, and his pose dominates the stage. He has the
ability to metamorphose from being a gentle and humorous individual to an angry one with ease. In this play all these qualities
are expressed.'

While at the Albery, there was the incident of an extremely
worrying letter from a society that called itself 'Word Perfect'. It
was hand delivered to the stage door of the theatre and Michael
said it scared the bejabbers out of him. It was printed on Equity
stationery and looked incredibly official and authoritative.

The letter stated that both Equity and the Writers' Guild of
Great Britain had decided to tighten standards around textual
inaccuracies in order to maintain the total fidelity of plays put
on in the West End. Michael, because of his reputation, had
been selected as a guinea pig, and they were sending a member

of the committee with copies of the script of *Cressida* to follow the performance to see whether he was indeed 'word perfect'.

If he was not, there would be serious consequences: they threatened that if there were three digressions from the text an actor would be fined; if there were four, he would be banned from the profession. In addition, a report would be published in *The Stage*, so there would be total public humiliation as well. The letter was signed 'Dr Martin Aston'.

Michael was apoplectic.

'It's a fucking disgrace,' he railed, 'this is appalling, it's scandalous, the nerve,' and so forth, and of course he was naturally also very frightened. He found it increasingly difficult to remember lines and was well known for often giving himself free rein with the script.

Several nights later a call came through to his dressing room, telling Sir Michael there was a gentleman, a Dr Aston, who had been to see the show and would like to see him. Should he be shown to his room?

Sick with trepidation, Michael waited in his dressing room much like a condemned man in his cell, until the door opened.

To his relief, Dr Martin Aston turned out to be the actor Douglas Hodge, who was soon to play the role of Aston opposite Gambon in Harold Pinter's *The Caretaker*.

He said he could hear Simon Russell Beale, Terence Rigby, and many others 'laughing like a pack of fucking hyenas, the bastards – they had tricked me good and proper!' The trickster finally tricked.

23

'He cried at the end of every take'

Longitude, an adaptation of Dava Sobel's best-selling book, was written and directed by Charles Sturridge, with Michael playing the clockmaker John Harrison and Jeremy Irons the horologist Rupert Gould. This was an important film for Michael both professionally and personally. It was during filming that he met Philippa Hart, the mother of his sons Tom and Will.

The relationship between Sturridge and Michael was often quite strained and at times the cast and crew found it tough to witness. Michael had to do one scene thirty-two times – it was a long speech – he would hold his arms wide apart to describe the length and then cry at the end. Thirty-two takes.

On about take twenty, some of the row of extras behind his back started giggling uncomfortably, as you might expect at the absurdity and cruelty of the situation.

Bill Nighy went up to them between takes and said, 'If you laugh again during the take, I'll break your fucking heads off!'

They didn't laugh again.

Oliver Soden

Much has been written about his great outings, in Dennis Potter and Stephen Poliakoff on television, or in Brecht, Miller and Ayckbourn on stage.

I wish his role as the clockmaker John Harrison, in Charles Sturridge's *Longitude*, had been more praised. He was never better, and his were fingers that could easily have built maritime machines of such delicate complexity. When he lost his temper at the intransigent Board of Longitude, the power he conjured (vocal, emotional, physical) burned from the screen. (Cleopatra, on Antony: 'But when he meant to quail and shake the orb, he was as rattling thunder.') In a scene with Andrew Scott, during which Harrison is tempted to abandon his life's ambition, the tears rolled down his face, and a beleaguered soul shone through basset-hound eyes.

24

'I got my papers, you see. What I need is my papers. Then I can get down to Sidcup'

In 2001 he played what he described as 'an untrustworthy snake of a man – a brilliant character, a vagrant, a liar and a man desperately seeking validation and a place to belong, while simultaneously being completely incapable of taking responsibility for his own life' in Patrick Marber's revival of Pinter's *The Caretaker*. Davies's desire to get to Sidcup in the play is a recurring motif and a source of much ambiguity. Sidcup becomes a symbol of Davies's hopes and dreams. It represents a future where he is no longer a homeless, wandering vagrant. It's a place where he imagines he can finally settle down and find some peace. A place he can belong once he has his papers and can start working. Michael gave Davies a severe stoop to bring out his insinuating qualities. It occurred to him that if he made him the shabbiest, most physically repulsive man with a stoop and dressed in rags, it made it more amusing when he tries to assert his dignity and talk about Oxford.

For Michael this was a collaboration he did not enjoy. The rehearsal period was too relaxed for him. Patrick had a pool table moved into the space and Michael was unsettled by this: he said his nerves 'jangled'.

But then when I was in a moment of utter despair during rehearsals, you think, well, Harold says: 'Man sits on bed. He stands. He moves to the gas cooker. He gets out a penknife. He cuts his toenails.' Then you wonder – does this play even need a director? Whatever you do is there in that room. He almost tells you what to do. But of course, it does need a director. It does, it does, like mad. You feel as if the ship isn't floating properly: this isn't working. He shouldn't be there, I shouldn't be here, she shouldn't be there, this is all wrong.

Although he did admit with hindsight:

When the play opened, we had packed houses. I couldn't believe it, it was incredible. I liked Patrick but felt it lacked structure, and I worried that I'd let Harold down.

Rupert Goold directed Michael Gambon in another production of a Harold Pinter play, this time *No Man's Land* in 2008, produced by Michael Colgan, director of Dublin's Gate Theatre, and by Sonia Friedman in London. It was a sell-out success for its four-week run at the Gate before it transferred to the Duke of York, with a great cast consisting of Michael, who was a pitch-perfect Hirst, along with David Bradley, David Walliams and Nick Dunning.

Among the audience on opening night was a group of friends going to witness the performance, and to pay homage were a dying

Harold Pinter, Brian Friel and Rupert. Goold said the play 'passed through [Michael], like air through a flute'. At the end, both Pinter and Friel were on their feet, tears in their eyes, and it became obvious why writers revered him. As Rupert divined, 'I'm not sure if he entirely understood his genius, but then again perhaps that is one of its definitions.' This adds to the mystique surrounding his performance.

Good directors, like good writers, were essential for Michael's happiness and for his genius to flourish. Such a director was Robert Altman. *Gosford Park* was Altman's English murder mystery, an ensemble piece in which Michael played alongside Maggie Smith, Helen Mirren, Eileen Atkins, Kristin Scott Thomas, Kelly Macdonald and Emily Watson. He portrays Sir William McCordle, the imperious master who has invited distinguished company for a weekend shooting party before a murder throws everything into chaos.

Empire magazine declared the film 'Altman's best movie in years – an astute exploration of British culture that can stand proudly with his satires of American life. Atmospheric, absorbing, amusing and really fun.'

The film won the Bafta for Outstanding British Film and was nominated for six Academy Awards, including Best Picture.

Michael adored being in *Gosford Park*; he said it was like being on holiday. All the actors knew each other and had acted together before, and they used to come in even on their days off. They moved their caravans round into a circle like in a Western so they could have lunch together, share stories and have fun. Altman would sometimes cook for them. They had the sense of being a real family for the duration of the film.

Michael revered Altman:

What a director! He's the best; he's full of fun and jokes and games ... I was killed halfway through. It was upsetting. We used to ask Altman who had the lead, and he would say, 'I can't tell you.' It was great. It was a good part, that. A bit of a bastard! But he was working-class money. He wasn't of the manner born, was he? He kind of insinuated his way into their lives ... I loved the way he treats people. When Tom Hollander is trying to get me to help him set up a business, I just ignore him. I find that funny. It made me laugh.

Michael also recalled:

Altman gave me this yappy dog. I like dogs but I like big dogs and this one was smelly, awful. I didn't read the script so on the first day when Altman gave me this dog, I didn't want to admit that I didn't know about the dog, so I said, 'Oh, right.' And he gave me this dog, so I thought, how could I get Tom to take care of it, and so, I used to rough it up ... [*He mimed ruffling the dog's fur round and round*] until he got cross, and then I'd hand it to Tom and it would bite him! I thought that was very funny, poor bastard, and left him having to hold it. But I was stuck with it most of the time.

Michael told me a classic story from the first day of principal shooting, when, as ever, he had not read the script properly. He cast his eye round the room, and proceeded to wink and blow kisses at Maggie Smith throughout the take.

When the take ended, Maggie asked Michael why he was blowing kisses and making googly eyes at her. He told her that he thought it was appropriate, as they were playing husband and wife. Looking at him like he was mad she said, 'I'm not playing your wife you bloody idiot: Kristin is playing your wife!'

Robert Altman's directorial style was remarkable for its collaborative and improvisational nature. He fostered a relaxed and supportive atmosphere on set, encouraging actors to develop their characters and dialogue beyond the confines of the script. This was ideal for Michael as he would be given loose outlines and scenarios which helped and encouraged him to work organically and contribute to the overall narrative. Altman's inspired approach resulted in a naturalistic and unpredictable quality, where he really succeeded in capturing the nuances, flaws and foibles of human interaction, which gives his films a deep authenticity and truth. He completely trusted his actors, and this was something Michael loved about working with him, plus his meticulous planning of the technical aspects. He often spoke admiringly about Altman's directing style:

What he liked to do was have three cameras running on tracks. He'd have a very complicated scene with ten people in it and by lunchtime he's done it. He would give you freedom to do things and I thought it was a nice thing to do. I loved that freedom. I'd even make up lines, and he'd use them. I would say, 'Well, you wouldn't know what someone was going to say if you walked into a room.'

25

'I am old, I am old'

Path to War (2002) is a film about the Vietnam War as
seen through the eyes of the then president of the United
States, Lyndon B. Johnson, and his cabinet. Michael said that
as he read more about Johnson and got to understand him, he
wished that he'd met him, and believed that, if it hadn't been
for Vietnam, Johnson would have been a great president. Even
though he pretended on countless occasions that he did no
preparation, he confided in an interview that:

I liked the sound of Lyndon Johnson. I liked to listen to
the Oval Office tapes when he was ringing up his tailor in
Chicago, wanting to have some new pants made, saying,
'These pants cut my nuts.' ... He says, 'On the five pairs of
pants I want you to make, I want more room for my nuts
and deeper pockets for my money. And also my knife.' ...
That's amazing. The President of the United States wants to
carry loose change in his pocket ... He was deeply impressed
by Harvard and Yale men who sat around him, and he just

listened to them, McNamara and all those people. It's a sad story. And then as soon as he left, he died – within four years … We started working [on the film] just after 9/11. We delayed a week because of that. Flying there to play an American president after that happened it made it worse.

Michael was invited to the French embassy in Washington for a screening of *Path to War* but spent the duration of the film chain-smoking in the lobby. After the film, many of the audience, including old congressmen and senators, were in tears. Jack Valenti, the president of the Motion Picture Association of America, was also crying. He had once worked as a special assistant to President Johnson, and was also present in the motorcade when John F. Kennedy was assassinated in Dallas.

Having immersed himself in the weighty world of Lyndon B. Johnson, Michael was ready for a break, and when the film wrapped he decided to visit the set of *Doctor Zhivago*, which was being filmed by Granada Television in Prague. On the crew were several friends, and Philippa Hart was in the art department.

PHILIPPA HART

Michael came out to visit Prague, and three members of the crew had worked on *The Singing Detective* with him. It was agreed between the four of them that, as that day they were filming a big crowd scene in the train station, costume would dress him in a large heavy overcoat and Russian hat. It was too good an opportunity not to use. The camera operator knew Michael's position on the platform as he was on the moving train filming the crowds of people waiting to get onto it. As he approached

Michael, the camera zoomed in on him. Cut to the rushes being watched in London by the producers at LWT, and one of them said, 'Can you rewind that sequence, as I'm pretty sure that was Michael Gambon in the crowd of extras ...'

––––––––––––––––

In 2003, Michael appeared in the television adaptation of the celebrated Tony Kushner play *Angels in America*, directed by Mike Nichols. He adored the experience because Nichols was a legendary figure, and both Al Pacino and Meryl Streep were in it, and also because it is a phenomenal piece of art.

Michael and Simon Callow both played angels:

> We get dressed in nightshirts and we have funny hair, funny faces with weird make-up and we stand around the bed with the guy dying of AIDS. They said to us, this moment you turn around and you see the stage coming up hydraulically out of the floor and a staircase going up to heaven. And the two young actors embrace and start dancing to 'Moon River'. And I watched this. The camera's on us, and I couldn't stop crying. Nice music, and two of the most beautiful young men in the world. And the story of the play, and Tony Kushner, and AIDS.

Shakespeare's *Henry IV Parts I and II*, directed by Nicholas Hytner at the National Theatre in 2005, was difficult for Michael. Tragically, it was not his finest hour, and by the last weeks critics and audiences alike agreed. Indeed, it was during this production that his fading memory became increasingly pronounced, and as his insecurity and fear was exchanged for more clowning, it all became a little baroque, the fat suit grew

larger, the clarity of his lines was blurred. This was a foreshad-
owing of what was to come. At moments he seemed lost and
blundered around adding indulgent bits of business, including a
scene in which he managed to pee up a tree, reaching its topmost
branches. The life force and humour of Falstaff one could take
for granted; it was his sadness, his chimes-at-midnight mortality
that lingered, one critic wrote, as when, rejected by Hal – 'I know
thee not, old man' – his enormous body seemed to sag, deflate,
and then fold in half.

In Part II, Falstaff meets the prostitute Doll Tearsheet, played
by Eve Myles.

'I am old, I am old,' he tells her.

'I love thee better than I love e'er a scurvy young boy of them
all,' Doll replies.

In this there was a marvellous tenderness and heartbreaking
moment of deep affection between these two lost souls.

MATTHEW MACFADYEN

[In] only my second or third television job, we played father and
son in Stephen Poliakoff's *Perfect Strangers*. It was a wonderful
cast – Lindsay Duncan, Timothy Spall et al., but I couldn't quite
believe I was acting with Michael. And he was just so warm and
lovely: wicked, elegant, twinkling, soulful, rackety. We had a
few weeks of night shoots at Claridge's early on and we'd stand
outside on Brook Street at 3 a.m., smoking, me utterly enthralled
and weak with laughter. [...]

He was so kind, too. I had to cry in a take at one point, as I
watched his character (as my dad) drunkenly making a fool of
himself at a family reunion. Michael wasn't on camera, but he saw
that I was nervous and came over very discreetly and quietly to

talk to me and encourage me. I was overwhelmingly moved by that. So of course my tears just flowed in the take.

In 2005 we played Hal and Falstaff at the National, in Nick Hytner's production of *Henry IV, I and II* – another father/son relationship of sorts. Again such fun, but a little wobbly with the lines, a little more rackety. I could sense a nervousness in him. It's exhilarating playing those great big canonical roles but frightening too. There'd been a good deal of silliness among the cast throughout the run – water balloon fights before each show in the internal courtyard space of the National. But I won't forget those flashes of fear in his eyes, standing with him in the wings of the Olivier stage, waiting to go on.

Elliot Levey, in an article for the *Guardian*, described his experiences of the production. Having the Great Gambon as Falstaff was, as he described it, 'front-page news'. Nick Hytner's interpretation conflated several of the more ancient lords into the role of Westmoreland, which brought Elliot into the orbit of the mischievous Lord of Misrule, Falstaff. It was here that Elliot experienced the power of Michael's creativity and endless ability to play. He also witnessed first hand the reverence Michael held for outstanding performance when John Wood was there: 'John Wood scared the bejesus out of [Michael]. He was scary, the great intellectual Shakespearean with a famously quick temper. He was then diminished with emphysema but still had astonishing power even when forced to use his falsetto. Gambon suddenly had to try hard. He stopped his insouciance and raised his game.'

It was, as Matthew Macfadyen acknowledged, the Rogues' Company, where they were permanently wet from water bombing not just each other, but every other actor in the building.

This anarchy proved to be particularly painful for the cast of other productions, who had to walk on stage in dripping-wet Restoration wigs and costumes.

For Elliot and the others involved, this was the riotous and anarchic energy of Shakespeare's original company of King's Men. It certainly helped develop an enormous camaraderie among the company.

By this time, Michael had inherited the role of Dumbledore in Harry Potter. As a consequence, he visited a dentist in Harley Street, who fitted him with a brand-new set of titanium teeth. Elliot noted that the production benefited hugely from this, as his voice suddenly became clear again. Of course, what wasn't as evident was the agony behind the buffoonery, the anxiety, and the growing fear that he would not remember his lines.

26

'I'm sick of these dolphins. They're always swimming around'

By December 2003 Michael was in Rome, working on the Wes Anderson film *The Life Aquatic with Steve Zissou*. He also worked with Anderson on *Fantastic Mr. Fox* (2009). Michael respected Wes hugely and loved working on his films.

When Michael was interviewed about his career at this time, he said that he viewed his career 'as a moveable feast, well, more moveable than feast'.

But feast it certainly was, and Michael was working like a fiend; he loved it, he craved it, it gave him the essential nourishment he needed as an artist.

For Michael, Ireland was a sacred place, and whenever he worked there he felt hugely inspired. One particularly happy period was filming the noir crime TV series *Quirke* with Gabriel Byrne, who played the titular character, a pathologist in 1950s Dublin. Gambon played the corrupt Judge Garret Griffin, a bigshot in

Dublin society; once again he delighted in taking on the challenge of playing a despicable character involved in an orphanage siphoning babies from Ireland to wealthy American families in Boston. A complicated, dark and villainous man.

He hugely respected Byrne and enjoyed his company. And as always when he was in Dublin he also spent a great deal of time off-set with the producer at the Gate Theatre, Michael Colgan, talking about new productions of Beckett they wanted to stage, especially *Eh Joe*, which was presented at the Edinburgh Festival with Penelope Wilton to great applause. A performance that Michael was always extremely proud of.

Another cherished time filming in Ireland was on the set of Deborah Warner's *The Last September*. Michael often spoke about Deborah with great reverence and said how much he respected her talent as a director:

> I love her, she is excellent. Great clarity. No bullshit. *Last September*, which we shot in Ireland, we had proper rehearsal time – six weeks' shooting near Dublin, which was fabulous. Plus, she's the most attractive woman I know. She's mind-bogglingly attractive. I can hardly breathe. Just her being, the way she sits, the way she talks, I find her altogether overwhelming.

Deborah said of Michael, 'What a heavenly flirt. But the seduction was his acting – got me every time. He was a true genius. The essence of actor. The best.' She recalled:

> In *Last September* I gave him one of the first electricity generators to play with in his role in the film. He was terribly happy. That's what he needs. He's a precision engineer ... He needs

to be entertained. All those big brain actors do – Maggie [Smith], Fiona [Shaw] or him. They absolutely need to be fed. They're tigers . . . He and Maggie have marvellous reputations of being tricky and they are not at all. They just have to be fed.

She also said, 'He loved my skin – so he said – always flattering, but especially so from him.'

Deborah added that, towards the end of the shoot, Michael was longing to return to the theatre after all his film work, and was looking forward to working with Matthew Warchus again, on Beckett's *Endgame*.

He was always very fond of quoting Nell's line from the play, 'Nothing is funnier than unhappiness, I grant you that,' and he would then shake his head sagely before laughing uproariously.

In the 2004 production at the Albery, Michael played Hamm, the blind and immobile master, alongside Lee Evans as Clov, his servant. Their relationship is one marked by dependence, resentment and a darkly comedic power dynamic. Hamm is completely reliant on Clov yet treats him with not just disdain but cruelty. Clov, in turn, is bound to Hamm in a Stockholm-syndrome scenario but longs to leave.

Lee was a well-established and successful performer with experience in stand-up, film and theatre. *Endgame* was a different kind of role for him, showcasing his dramatic abilities in a challenging and serious play, and he was anxious before the curtain rose and had to beg Michael not to corpse him.

Michael, of course, was at his playful best, with Beckett's genius to weave his magic and a wheelchair contraption that was a complete death trap. He thought Lee was brilliant and loved their time together, confident that he would have the courage to 'take it on', as he said. The production was breathtaking, a dazzling helter-skelter *tour de force*. Matthew Warchus's big regret, like so many other great directors, was that he wished he could have worked with him more. He adored the extraordinary musicality of Michael's virtuosic interpretation: 'bassooning of the word "hollow"' and his delicious, 'soft, deep cello sound of this disconcerting "You're a bit of alright, aren't you?"' in his oul' Dubs drawl.

Lee's hilarious and generous account of the opening night is a raw, warts and all portrayal of what it was like for him to enter the bravura and mayhem of Michael's rollercoaster Beckettian world.

LEE EVANS

A condemned man waiting on the gallows about to be hanged has at least a fair crack, a faint hope, that at the last desperate moment a bearer on horseback might gallop forth through the baying mob brandishing aloft a note of reprieve in order that:

'This madness must stop!'

Well, there's no such hope where I'm standing.

Tonight is the opening performance of Sonia Friedman's production of Samuel Beckett's exuberantly jolly play, *Endgame*.

Starring myself as Clov, the bumbling buffoon, not such a big leap for my acting skills, one might suggest, however cast alongside perhaps one of Britain's greatest and most celebrated actors, the revered Sir Michael Gambon in the role of Hamm, my acting skills at this moment in time had been pushed into a more method portrayal of someone suffering with petrified paralyses.

Meanwhile Sir Michael sat serene, a zen-like master, seemingly laser-focused on the task at hand. Having calmly assumed his position on the other side of the stage, he appeared a steady,

but highly coiled spring, sitting as he was in a wheelchair leaning forwards, in the traps, ready, focused, staring straight ahead
gripping each armrest so tightly it made his fists look like he was
wearing a row of ball bearings as knuckle dusters on each hand.
The great Gambo was a caged bear.

Michael's wheelchair was a contraption that he, along with
the props department, had spent weeks conspiring and design-
ing to ergonomically fit his character, Hamm. But from where I
was standing it resembled a pile of refuse that had been thrown
together from an illegal fly-tip.

One particular section of its construction was a certain
supermarket trolley, wobbly wheel, spiteful bastard bit, that,
because it hated me, would at every performance for nineteen solid weeks while I was pushing the hefty Sir Michael
in it, without any discernible reason just veer the fuck off at
a keen forty-five-degree angle across the stage and into the
wings, transforming what had been the highly regarded classic
play *Endgame* into 'Cirque du Soleil starring the terrified Sir
Michael Gambon' being flung about by what looked like his
carer, the gormless, limping half-wit Lee Evans, a nightly rou-
tine that prompted Michael, while desperately trying to remain
in character, to enquire,

'Where da hell are we goin', Evans? It's not fuckin' *Top Gear!*'

Something that struck me upon meeting other actors, co-
medians, producers or directors was, as soon as I mentioned I
was working with 'Michael Gambon' they would each enter a
trance-like state, their head tilting gently to one side as their eyes
glazed over with melancholy as if some fond distant recollection
had entered their mind. Most striking of all was watching their
faces change as they spoke, their expressions gradually forming
into the broadest, brightest smile before launching into their own

priceless yarn about Michael and of how they themselves had the best time working with him.

However, what was most striking was each person would always sign off with the same cautionary reminder that, despite Michael's notorious, endless and hilarious spinning of stories, his jokes, impersonations and seemingly playful, childlike, cuddly demeanour, there was when it finally came down to it, when you found yourself standing next to him on an actual stage and the lights go up, that's when it will hit you harder than a flying anvil and you realise 'This bloke, they would caution, is the real fucking deal.'

It was roughly two minutes before the curtain rises and at this point I was beginning to feel desperate for any human reassurance and so in a reckless moment of despair and in the hope I wouldn't disturb Michael too much, I whispered politely across the stage towards where he was sitting:

'Fuck me, Michael, I'm not sure if I can go through with this shit.'

There was no reaction. Nothing: he just sat there quietly staring forward, serene, a monk-like figure perched at the ready on the edge of his wheelchair seat, but then suddenly, without looking at me, he spoke.

His voice, already in character, was soft, a gentle Irish brogue with a deep, penetrating baritone, as if an old bow was slowly being drawn across the strings of a mature double bass, every syllable pronounced with exact clarity as if they were delivered politely right next to my ear.

'Can you hear that?' he said. I was confused. 'Can I hear *them*? The audience. Gathering on the other side of the curtain, is that what . . . ? 'No! Can you hear it?' he demanded.

I tried listening more intently. Maybe there was something I was unaware of going on? I mean, I'm not an actor, so . . .

Then something encouraging struck me. Was lady luck perhaps about to pay me a visit? Michael's little relapse into hearing voices could be my ticket out of here. I'm saved! He was hearing things!

'Michael?' I enquired over-sympathetically, as one might address an outpatient in a psychiatric ward before turning up the morphine drip. 'I would quite understand if you didn't want to . . .'

'No! Listen!' he snapped loudly, cutting me off.

Immediately I made a big display of listening, straining my ears, joining him in an overly dramatic but keen desire and expectation of hearing at least something, given his apparent irritable tone.

But, alas, there was nothing. What was going on? The play was about to begin and he was hearing stuff. I was just beginning to feel like Sancho Panza when Michael surprisingly raised a finger in the air and with that . . .

Let forth the most horrendous, walloping, drawn-out, entire woodwind section of a fart; the length and decibel of which resembled that of a giant walrus passing a tuba and unnaturally seemed to thunder on for what was an un-biological, even biblical amount of time. I watched with astonishment as eventually it appeared to tail off into a high-pitched sort of strangled, rat-sounding squeak in which Michael took great pleasure in accompanying by joyfully flicking his index finger into the air in order to conduct the last tiny remnants of the farting concerto, as if it had some *Last Night of the Proms* connotation.

Astonished, I stared at him, my stony shock only stoking his reaction, which was to suddenly burst into a howling, uncontrollable fit of laughter, only pausing for a brief moment to check in with me and noticing my expression hadn't changed only seemed to make him explode all the more into rapturous, aching pleasure, as he rocked back and forth in his chair clasping at his sides in agony.

In the production my character, Clov, is a pitiful, wretched mutt, a mongrel. Described by Beckett himself as 'a brute and a beast'. A deformed figure who wore clothes stained with piss and excrement, he has matted hair that hangs down across a deformed, mangled, filthy, disease-ridden face incorporating a reached hole, a swirling gob that's devoid of teeth.

So there I am, waiting, about to open in London's glittering West End all dressed up like a public toilet brush, watching the classically trained Sir Michael Gambon laughing like a child at his own enormous and most hideous of farts. Just then Michael stopped laughing, turned and, after carefully scrutinising me from head to toe, remarked seriously:

'Can I just say Evans, seeing you standing there and looking like you do, it really is absolutely inspired casting. And by the way,' he added, 'you really should ask if you can have that costume when the play ends coz it dun arf suit ya.'

Michael also had a charming, almost childlike sense of pleasure in trying to make you laugh during a performance, wherever an opportunity arose. He delighted whenever there was a pause in the play, a gap he might exploit by pulling a few low-key faces at you while gleefully knowing he wouldn't be seen by the audience, or mumbling something under his breath in your direction in order to put you off your stride.

But the number one caper I found most entertaining was, if he was performing his big solo, his monologue, and halfway through some unsuspecting, but mostly, in his view, mindless audience member coughed, that was the trigger for Michael and he would immediately stop talking, his brows would lock together and he would throw the offending area of the audience a boiling, discerning glare, then, after a moment, he would proceed all the way back to the beginning and start again, and if the cougher in question should cough again during that speech, Michael would stubbornly go back yet again and start afresh from the beginning, leaving the audience with no clue as to what was going on. It being of course Sir Michael Gambon, it must surely be part of the play. Michael once jokingly informed me after a performance, 'Most of those people out there simply have no idea what the play is all about in the first place.' 'In fact,' he would say, leaning forward in his dressing-room chair and lowering his voice to a conspiratorial whisper, 'between you and me, I don't even frickin' understand it meself and I'm in it!' After which he'd erupt into a huge roar of laughter, rolling backwards and flinging his great hands in the air.

So as I stood there waiting for my fate, the great Gambo by my side, I wondered to ask him:

'Michael, do you really think I can do this?'

'You have been brought to this spot, Evans,' he said firmly, one of his famous long fingers jabbing down towards the stage, 'for a reason, and I wouldn't be here if I thought we couldn't do it, so let's show them.'

Emboldened, I was overcome with a sudden surge of confidence, his words having ignited a fire that roared my flames of self-belief. I was ready!

'Yes! Let's do it,' I enthused, pounding the air with my fist.

While he sat solemnly, his gaze fixed straight ahead as he murmured from out of the side of his mouth, his words deep, dark and foreboding.

'May God have mercy on your soul!'

'This,' he said firmly, 'will be the best thing you have ever done, EVANS.'

'Yes? Why?' I asked.

'Coz I'm in it.'

And with that the curtain whipped open.

We came to a rest on the other side of the play, safely back behind the curtain, to the muffled roar of the crowd.

I found him standing a few feet away from me, his face beaming with anticipation, appearing desperate to hear how I felt about my first night in the West End.

'Well?'

'Blimey, Michael, that was amazing.'

'Good. Now that's over with, can I just say ...

'Whatever disease you have mentally, I think it impossible to beat with any conventional treatment.'

And with that he turned and swept away.

27

'Every part I play is just a variant of my own personality'

Michael would say that he 'didn't feel the need to deeply research or prepare for roles, just relied on his own instincts', and in an interview given in 2007 he famously said of the heavily bearded role of Dumbledore, which was fun to play but unrepresentatively twinkly, 'I just stick on a beard and play me, so it's no great feat.'

The phenomenon that is Harry Potter provided Michael with a fabulous vehicle to exhibit his gifts as a magician and to exploit his playfulness and childlike qualities.

Dumbledore wasn't originally his role. He inherited the character from the great Richard Harris and to journalists he was always self-deprecating about playing him. Alfonso Cuarón personally selected Michael for *Harry Potter and the Prisoner of Azkaban* (2004), and Michael portrayed the character in five more films, concluding with *Harry Potter and the Deathly Hallows Part 2* in 2011.

I asked him about the character after he'd had a chance to properly percolate and process it, and he said that he truly felt that the headmaster of Hogwarts was 'arguably the most complex character in the Harry Potter series. He is a figure of immense power, wisdom and moral ambiguity who embodies both human nature's light and dark sides.'

Michael's perspective on Dumbledore was that he could also be quite scary. He said, 'All headmasters should be a bit scary, shouldn't they? A top wizard like him would be intimidating. And ultimately, he's protecting Harry. Essentially, I play myself. A little Irish, a little scary. That's what I'm like in real life.'

His debut in *Harry Potter and the Prisoner of Azkaban* imbued the character with a darker, always mischievous tone – Michael felt he was more Merlin. He was a tougher, patriarchal figure, with more urgency and a mysterious force amid an impending war. Many preferred the more twinkling gentleness, the more cuddly, softer character that Harris brought.

This was something that resonated hugely with Michael, who was an immensely complicated character. For him, Dumbledore's other facet or gift was that he was a brilliant strategist, always several steps ahead of his opponents. He meticulously planned his moves with a chess player's agility, anticipating Voldemort's actions and manipulating events to achieve his aims.

In *Harry Potter and the Order of the Phoenix*, Dumbledore sets intricate plans to protect Harry, and Michael performed his calculated use of prophecy with devastating and dazzling effect.

Dumbledore was also, for Michael, something of a beacon of morality, mostly embodying the values of love, compassion and selflessness. 'He prioritises the greater good, even when it means he needs to make decisions and choices that, when presented, may appear morally ambiguous. His strong moral compass regarding Harry, alongside his unwavering belief in Harry's potential, means that his ultimate self-sacrifice is for the greater good,' he would say when looking back on his role.

He felt that Dumbledore carried a significant burden of knowledge, both personal and historical:

He is completely immersed in wizardry and has a thorough and complex sense of the nature of good and evil based on his experience, scholarship and talent. Of course, like us all he is also flawed, despite his brilliance and noble intentions. His past mistakes and romantic involvement with Grindelwald haunt him and further contribute to his multifaceted personality and complicated character. He can also be manipulative and secretive, sometimes prioritising his own goals and desires over the wellbeing of others. He inspires those around him with his unwavering belief in the power of love and the importance of fighting for what is right.

How like Michael, I would think, and I understood completely why he needed to play this role at this stage in his life and career. It was in part a great revelation of himself.

It was also a source of great amusement to Michael that, after a career of playing sadists, malcontents and great Shakespearean anti-heroes, what comes up when you google him these days is pages of Harry Potter fan mania, analysing his role as Dumbledore.

He would bemoan the fact that 'I should be one of the villains. The other actors are terrific: Tim Spall, Gary Oldman, David Thewlis, a really strong group of actors.'

True to form, Michael did not read the books and firmly believed that the magic of the wizarding world was more in the script, on the set and within the environment they created, not in the source material.

'You'd get upset about all the scenes it's missing from the book, wouldn't you? ... No point in reading the books because you're playing with [screenwriter] Steve Kloves's words.'

Jokingly he referred to the Harry Potter experience as entering his third act, his wizard phase, a lineage alongside other great actors that includes Alec Guinness (as the powerful wizard-like Jedi Obi-Wan Kenobi in *Star Wars*) and Ian McKellen (as Gandalf in *Lord of the Rings*).

Of course, his secret, his genius, was that he always trusted his internal compass, listening to that little voice that navigated him towards the truth; what Sir Ralph Richardson had noticed and shared: living in a dream-like state, he made the role his own, donning the long silver beard and half-moon spectacles and speaking in his unmistakable rich baritone. From the very first moment he arrived on set, he broke the Harris tradition of Dumbledore. Despite the director's protestations, he ran up the stairs and instantly claimed the role, becoming his unique interpretation of the headmaster of Hogwarts.

Michael adored playing alongside Alan Rickman – as Professor Snape – and considered him a great friend, a brilliant and generous individual and a real man of the theatre and the stage.

ALAN RICKMAN

As a drama student and a schoolboy I was sitting in the cheap seats watching Maggie Smith and Michael Gambon at the National Theatre, so to then find yourself working with them, them becoming friends and, of course, Michael has the wickedest sense of humour and Maggie is one of the wittiest people alive, I only regret I didn't have a tape recorder or a notebook or could do shorthand, you can't compete with those two, that was so fun.

Rickman had already been diagnosed with prostate cancer before filming *Harry Potter and the Order of the Phoenix*. His death was a great loss to everyone, and Michael especially missed him.

It was only at the London premiere of *Half-Blood Prince*, where more than four thousand children turned up to glimpse the magical cast, that Michael felt that the enormity of the Potter phenomenon truly hit him. He said it was both heart-warming and bittersweet:

> The number of children there really moved me. It was pouring with rain, and everyone was getting drenched; some had been there for hours.
>
> You felt responsible for them in a way. All their books and pieces of autograph paper were wet; the pens wouldn't work. It was so sad. It makes you think how big this thing is. It's been a real privilege.

David Yates, who directed the last four films, described Michael as a mischievous, playful, yet also deeply thoughtful actor who brought a 'memorable, subversive, soulful' Dumbledore to the screen while also being enormous fun on set: pragmatic, accessible, funny and down to earth, and who, despite his immense talent, effortlessly made all the younger actors around him feel at ease.

Another very special part of being in the Potter family for

so long was having the opportunity to watch Daniel Radcliffe, Emma Watson and Rupert Grint grow up; they were especially fun for him and he adored them.

'They've become worldly-wise and strong actors. That's been nice to see. You can say things you couldn't say to them now.'

One of his most famous pranks on set was with Alan Rickman when they successfully planted a fart machine inside Daniel Radcliffe's sleeping bag when the entire school was sleeping in the great hall, and Daniel had managed to manoeuvre himself to lie in his bag next to a girl he fancied. During a tranquil and intense moment – Daniel moved in his bag – Michael operated the machine with devastating effect.

Ralph Fiennes, who played Voldemort, paid tribute after his death: 'Michael Gambon was a tower of an actor – an irreplaceable force. His Galileo is branded on my memory. He defined theatre acting for a generation. What a loss.'

Fiennes had also acted with Michael in *The Master Builder* in 1995, so they were long-time colleagues and friends, with a mutual love of the theatre and of being part of a company:

I was talking to Ralph Fiennes the other night, and he said, his greatest joy is being in a theatre and being part of a company. I think it's mine as well, being with a group of people. I miss that. That's what I admire about Ralph. He's a movie star but he keeps on doing these big plays . . . I think his movies finance his theatre career. I like his bravery [in Ibsen's *Brand*]. I like the way he stands on the stage with his feet foursquare and plays the part. It's a lovely simple production by Adrian Noble – there's no bullshit about it . . . Ralph got a bit of humour in there as well, which was clever . . . I have to do two other Harry Potter movies after this. It's like having a bit of a

pension. So I could do a bit more theatre. I was thinking: I'd
like to find a really good new play and go to Michael Codron
or Robert Fox and say, will you put this on? ... For once, I
would just like to control my life ... You want something
from the heart that's lying unused on some desk. Some great
work of art.

NICK ALLOTT

Adrian, Mike and I took Ralph and his then girlfriend out to
dinner after the three of us had been to see Ralph in *God of
Carnage*. Essentially, we were all chatting away and Ralph, as
ever, was quite taciturn. Mike was getting a little bit bored, and
at one point Ralph turned to him and said, 'So, Michael, what
have you been doing today?'

And Mike said, 'Well, to be honest with you, Ralph, I got
killed!'

And Ralph said, 'Oh, I'm sorry to hear that.'

And Michael said, 'Basically, I had to climb up the top of this
tower, so I climbed to the top of this tower.'

And he got louder and LOUDER, and as he told this story
he climbed onto the table. He climbed up and demonstrated
the whole climb up the tower. And then he got to the top, and
he said – 'and when I got to the top, I got pushed off, and I
went – OhhhhArggggghhhhheeerhhhhhhhhhherrrrr'.

And he made this incredible noise of him falling, and by now,
of course, the entire restaurant was absolutely riveted by the sight
of the great man performing for us. We were all in hysterics.

'And then I went SLAP BANG at the bottom.'

And Ralph said to him, 'Who pushed you off?'

'You did, you CUNT. Don't you read your script?'

28

*'Think of a face, Joe, a face like
yours, when you were young'*

Beckett's thirty-minute play *Eh Joe*, about a man endlessly
forced to confront his past, with echoes of *Krapp's Last
Tape*, was one of Michael's proudest moments. He loved this
piece.

Atom Egoyan's staging at Dublin's Gate Theatre had him as
an elderly man alone, in a bare monastic room, who is clearly
afraid of something unseen. His hands tremble as he moves
about the cell enacting his habitual twilight ritual. We see him
lock the cupboard and look under the bed. Like a terrified child,
he needs to check for monsters. Only once he is satisfied that he
is safe can he sit perched on his bed. But he is not safe and has
created his own prison, his sealed room in which he cannot now
escape his past.

Penelope Wilton's disembodied voice starts to attack him.
It is an insidious act of revenge in the voice of a discarded lover
and she quietly and deliberately takes her revenge not only

for her betrayal but for all the other women he has betrayed. A screen comes down and Michael sits perfectly still with his face projected in a giant close-up on the screen, allowing us to scrutinise the impact every word is having on him, his face becoming a landscape of utter desolation until a single tear courses down his face. It is an incredible tour de force: a man, a seducer who used words to entrap his victims, is now being tormented by them.

After one performance of *Eh Joe* at the Gate, an earnest American academic started grilling Michael about his character's motivations. What did he think his character was doing on stage? Without missing a beat and utterly deadpan, Michael replied, 'Watching *EastEnders*.'

Eh Joe came to mean so much to Michael, needing, he would say, to 'atone'. It was a play he so wanted to perform again. No words, just summoning his incredible range, focus and mastery of his craft and experience.

He felt he reached a state of absolute purity, but he also said it cost him. It was cruel that he was achieving such amazing new heights as his memory was increasingly failing him, and I thought how it's impossible to reach the impossible without suffering.

In 2009 Michael was twice rushed to A & E at St Thomas' Hospital in London from rehearsals after suffering panic attacks.

The following year he performed *Krapp's Last Tape*, arguably Beckett's masterpiece, as though he was the last man on earth.

He has a sad clown's face and clawlike hands. A derelict waistcoat, torn shirt, shoes reduced to shells in which he shuffles about the room alone in the dark with a writing desk, overhead lamp and two bananas in a drawer. His only company is some dusty books and an antediluvian tape recorder and tapes. 'Spool,' he croons, like a mating call out in the void.

Here he is shipwrecked. Desolate, finished before he has started, a brilliant portrayal and a heartbreakingly portentous view into his future.

OLIVER SODEN

It is his fingers I will remember. Longer than they had any right to be, they were both brutish and graceful, as capable of wringing a neck as of drawing an elegant shape upon the air. As Krapp, in Beckett's monologue, *Krapp's Last Tape*, keeping a surreptitious eye on the script that, from my upper-circle seat, I could see clearly open on the table before him, he let one finger drag slowly along the carving of the desk's edge, as if playing a guiro.

Elisabeth Frink once made an etching of Michael Gambon as Antony (Helen Mirren was Cleopatra), and let his enormous hands become the largest thing in the picture, dangling at its centre with nails as large as eyes. Frink was the right artist: Gambon's was a face carved and hewn rather than born or made, comparable, in its delicate bulk, to one of her monumental heads.

Contradiction was perhaps the essence of his greatness, and he played upon it, hiding an evident seriousness and intellect, to say nothing of prowess at classical guitar and his crafting of replica antique weaponry, beneath the persona of one who didn't really know what this acting lark was all about. He did, and worked at it (as his co-stars testify) with technique and determination.

29

'I'm sorry, Johnny. I should have told you. I thought I was protecting you'

E ven as Michael's memory started to deteriorate, his power-ful voice was still in high demand. Most notably, he became the voice of HSBC bank.

In 2010 he asked me to be his earwig on *Page Eight*, written and directed by David Hare. This role involves feeding lines to the actor live during the scene. Some actors prefer having their lines delivered this way as it keeps them fresh. For Michael, it was to help him focus on the scene without panicking he might forget them. It was an incredible experience, and Michael was able to return to his former glory which was mesmerising for us all. This was the start of our working life together.

DAVID HARE

He had a useful sideline in voice-overs, usually doing what he called his 'posh voice'. It was that slight distance between the boy from the working-class Dublin family and the characters he played that gave him a distinctive edge of veiled imposture. In Pinter, he used the posh voice to scare the hell out of you.

He appeared in *Page Eight*, a spy film that is still happily trending on Netflix ... He played the head of MI5. One night we shot a long scene in which he apologises to Johnny Worricker, the central character, played by Bill Nighy, for not having trusted him more. I already knew from *Skylight* that shame, regret and a sense of honour were among Michael's strongest suits. But nobody could have foreseen the spell he cast over the entire crew who were pin-drop silent for two hours while he worked. At the end of the evening, Bill Nighy said that Michael had always been the only available pathfinder for a young actor aiming to do the job properly. Playing that scene with Michael, he said, was the supreme moment of his career.

Michael was not interested in award ceremonies or the hagiography that comes with fame and success. He cared deeply about the plays and especially the work of great playwrights such as Beckett, Hare, Gray, Friel, Churchill, Gill, Ayckbourn, Poliakoff, Miller, Albee and of course Pinter.

Michael demanded the audience's full attention and investment in the play. When he felt people were disinterested, unfocused or uninterested in great work, the famous 'red mist' would descend.

His temper, commingled with humour, was all part of 'the Great Gambon' mythology and Michael, when he was performing *All That Fall* at the Jermyn Street Theatre with Eileen Atkins (2012), and in Shaftesbury Avenue after *No Man's Land*, could be particularly fierce to autograph hunters hungrily armed with

Harry Potter memorabilia. 'Have any of you been to see the Beckett?' he would ask, the perpetual cigarette hanging from his mouth.

And if they hadn't, he would rage at them that they must as he had written magnificent plays – 'For fuck's sake' – that they should see. And then storm off.

All That Fall was written for radio, and Michael was able to have the script in front of him, which greatly helped because of his memory loss. Even so, it wasn't easy for him to always refer to the script during the performance. It was warmly received and to Michael's delight he and Eileen transferred to New York with it later that year.

30

'Watch out, Timex is here'

In July 2014, filming began for the television adaptation of J. K. Rowling's *The Casual Vacancy* in Gloucestershire and the south-west of England. The story unfolds following the sudden death of Barry Fairbrother, a popular and influential parish councillor, which throws the community into turmoil. His vacant seat on the council becomes a battlefield for various factions, exposing simmering tensions, secrets and lies. The cast was a brilliant ensemble including Rory Kinnear, Julia McKenzie, Keeley Hawes, Monica Dolan, Simon McBurney and Abigail Lawrie.

Michael played the preposterous Howard Mollison in a brilliant collaboration with Rufus Jones as his son Miles.

RUFUS JONES

One Friday night in Dean Street, Soho, 6.30 p.m., summer of 2014, I get a call from my agent. The job's yours. I don't know why I remember the place and time so specifically. Who am I kidding? The series was J. K. Rowling's *The Casual Vacancy*, and I was also told who was playing the other members of my fictional family. Married to Keeley Hawes, mothered by Julia McKenzie, manipulated by my tyrannical father – Michael Gambon.

Good God. Gambon.

Our first scene together, I was a puddle of nerves. And then, suddenly, Michael ruined a take by laughing at something I did. He pointed one of those vast fingers right at me, and roared, OH HE'S GOOD! It was like he'd flipped the petrol cap and filled me with a full tank of premium unleaded confidence.

I fell in love with him immediately.

Acting is such a strange thing – your heart receives the fictional ties with other actors at face value, and on-screen relationships can begin to feel strangely real. And not just between on-screen lovers. That summer, the Great Gambino became this gloriously daft, strangely noble surrogate father for me. And not just for me – for the entire production.

We filmed in the Cotswolds, all staying in the same Cheltenham hotel, every evening a pinch-me storm of dangerously late drinks in the bar. And at the eye of the storm, the Kubla Khan of this Gloucestershire Pleasure Dome. His nibs. The Great Gambino.

I forget who knighted him the Great Gambino. Possibly screenwriter Sarah Phelps and I spontaneously started calling him that. Why? Well, because he was. The Great Gambino was a different sort of magician from the headmasterly one he and Jo Rowling made so famous. This was a social magician, casting spells over us all with all the anecdotes that have been shared and reshared by a thousand giddy actors. Cigarettes speared into his huge ham-hock hands, conducting the words as he spoke them, a ring of smoke around him like the word wizard he was.

Regarding watchmaking, one day he asked me what watch I wore. I hesitated and pulled up my cuff. A Timex. It was a gift. TIMEX? FUCKING TIMEX??

That was my nickname for a week. WATCH OUT, TIMEX IS HERE.

But away from the grand storytelling, you occasionally got a peek behind the curtain, where the Great Gambino became Mike. And it was always a tantalising privilege. In the back seat with him on the way to set, he asked about my dad, who'd been diagnosed with Parkinson's. Dad was in the fringe world of physical theatre, a universe away from Mike's epic theatrical conquests. But he was fascinated, tender and supportive. We then started talking about our show, whose title he momentarily forgot. I asked him what he reckoned it should be called? He smiled and said, 'Avin' A Laugh'. He was bloody right, too.

Another moment that wrote itself on my memory. One night in a hotel in Bristol, he stayed up with me and a couple of others in the bar, regular shuttle runs together out to the smoking area. One time out there, a grandmother in her seventies sidled up to him and asked if he was famous? Mike shrugged. The lady then asked, well, would you write an autograph to my granddaughter, Josie? Mike found a piece of paper and a pen, and extremely carefully wrote: 'To Josie, Hello, All my love, Dumbledore x'. And then at the bottom in parentheses '(Michael Gambon)'. Know your audience, give them what they want. It was such a classy move.

31

'Where . . . where is Cordelia? My lines . . . I can't remember'

In early 2015, Michael made an announcement on the radio saying that he was leaving the stage, due to the increasing length of time, it was taking him to memorise his lines. He had previously tried being given prompts by theatre staff but found this unsatisfactory.

This was a heartbreaking moment. Especially as Tom Hollander, Sonia Friedman and I (his film and TV earwig) had been hoping to set up a production of *The Dresser* by Ronald Harwood. We attempted several rehearsals, using his earpiece device which worked well, but Michael became fearful of not being able to negotiate the stage and remember his lines.

He was terrified about what would happen if the connection broke and he couldn't hear his next line, or worse, and he would tell a funny story about another great actor, Michael Redgrave, who had an earpiece on stage in an Ibsen play and disastrously it somehow switched frequencies and tuned in to a local taxi firm. Unfortunately, during a very powerful scene he broke a profound moment of silence ... by suddenly announcing in a cockney accent, 'ARFUR, ARFUR ... can you go to Number 28 Battersea Rise and pick up a Mrs Hill? She's going to the bingo.'

32

'We are all born mad. Some remain so'

When Michael went to Dublin, which he did often either to read at the Gate or visit antique shops and friends, he would look out for productions of James Joyce's *Dubliners*, which he loved because he would say that the Irish realised Joyce's comedy and didn't make it portentous and dull. They could see that Joyce's writing contains elements of irony and satire that a delicate and nuanced approach could highlight, and bring to the forefront the absurdity, pretentions and hypocrisies of Dublin society. He also deeply appreciated the Irish theatre's understanding and interpretation of the comedy in Chekhov's works, which he found to be unique and refreshing.

But his absolute favourite was when he found an amateur, provincial production of *Waiting for Godot*. And he often recounted the story of the time he went out of Dublin to a small village hall to see it. He arrived early and was thrilled to discover that some people were already waiting to go inside. He passed the time standing outside with four old men sitting smoking and engaging in gentle banter. Until a stage manager came running out and cried to the men, 'Fellers, you're on.' Michael always said this was the greatest production of the play he ever witnessed. That seamless flow from the world onto the stage.

33

*'I'm a very boring person, so I like
to play interesting people'*

The television series *Fortitude* is a British psychological
thriller set in a fictional Arctic settlement in Svalbard.
The town of Fortitude, which boasts the lowest crime rate in
the world, is shattered by a brutal murder. As the investigation
unfolds, dark secrets and hidden agendas begin to surface.
The pristine façade of Fortitude begins to crumble, revealing
a sinister and complex web of relationships and scientific ex-
periments mutated and gone wrong. A terrifying prehistoric
parasite is emerging from the permafrost, threatening the entire
community.

The cast included Richard Dormer, Sofie Gråbøl, Stanley
Tucci, Christopher Eccleston and Phoebe Nicholls. Michael
played Henry Tyson, a renowned wildlife photographer particularly known for his stunning images of polar bears. He was
also suffering from a terminal illness, and so knew his time
was limited, which influenced his actions and decisions. It was

filmed in Iceland, and we were mainly based in Reyðarfjörður, a town in the east fjords with dramatic mountains and remote settlements; it was a tremendous adventure, with an amazing crew and hotel staff.

Michael was designated a couple of drivers: David, a photographer and an Englishman who had relocated to Iceland to marry a producer and raise a family, and Reynir, who is among other things one of Iceland's leading exponents of wrestling.

These two men became very dear friends of Michael's and mine. Many journeys into the frozen wastes were made entertaining, with Michael leading the singing of dirty songs from the infamous album by Peter Cook and Dudley Moore, *Derek and Clive (Live)*, which it soon became clear he knew off by heart. They delighted each other in tomfoolery and schoolboy smut.

Then Michael formed something of an obsession with the Icelandic writing legend Gunnar Gunnarsson, who had a remote farmhouse named Skriðuklaustur, and Michael insisted that he had heard a rumour that Gunnar had invited Adolf Hitler to play ping-pong at his retreat.

TGM, as David always affectionately referred to Michael (The Great Man, a moniker he never disputed), was instantly convinced that this had in fact been a cunning cover-up of a torrid homosexual affair complete with Nazi stormtroopers and regalia. (It all became an abiding obsession largely because there were few other distractions apart from visiting puffin colonies.)

So much so, that on our next day off the car was duly commandeered and we drove the four hours through endless tundra before arriving at the farm and museum of the great writer. Here we were greeted by a kind and bookish devotee who was delighted to have visitors and immediately treated us to some interminable silent films of Gunnar's oeuvre, including the *Meisterwerk*, *Guest* the One-Eyed, the first Icelandic book ever to have been made into a movie. David managed to extract Michael from the screening room with the excuse that a vital text had arrived.

TGM and David then mounted a full-scale search of the building, hunting for evidence of Hitler's part in the story. Although they could find no mention of Gunnarsson's dalliance with the Führer at the museum, mysteriously Michael did find photographs of Gunnar leaving Nazi headquarters in Berlin, as well as a letter from him to Hitler congratulating him on his splendid idea of invading Poland. Michael never revealed his sources as the provenance of the material – he just tapped his nose.

After about an hour the museum guide became suspicious, caught up with them and reprimanded them severely for wandering off unsupervised, so Michael asked him point-blank about the alleged relationship between the two parties and their mutual passion for table tennis.

This completely unnerved the guide, who muttered something about it not being a subject they really talked about. He said that he hadn't been aware of such a hobby and adamantly refused to expand on the ping-pong topic. All this served to convince Michael that as far as he was concerned, the rumours were true.

Later, over tea, Michael was further convinced that there had also been an incident in the sweet and extremely genteel museum café – and that he should re-enact it. Michael's behaviour took a strange turn, morphing into a disturbing blend of Hitler and Withnail as he demanded 'Cake, and the finest wines known to humanity!' The curator looked astonished, then disappeared. Much to our amazement – and the great hilarity of Michael – a cake appeared.

Strangely, a few days later Michael uncovered a book complete with a photo montage clearly showing the Führer in Lederhosen with a ping-pong bat. It was all to be kept very hush-hush and, as David often remarked affectionately, TGM never let the truth get in the way of a good story.

Stanley Tucci

When I was sent the script for *Fortitude* I asked my agents who else was in the cast. At that point there were two actors attached, Sofie Gråbøl and Michael Gambon. Upon hearing those names, I didn't care whether the script was good or bad because I would have happily just turned the pages in a reading of the dictionary if those two people were involved. Especially Michael Gambon. As a young actor I remember first seeing Michael in *The Cook, The Thief, His Wife & Her Lover* and being overwhelmed by his performance. He was magnetic, menacing, sexy and, of course, very funny. I think I learned more about acting from watching that performance than I did in four years of drama school. He was so assured, powerful and, most importantly, effortless. I saw him countless times after that in films and my experience was always the same. I was in awe. Upon seeing him on stage in *Skylight*, my awe was multiplied tenfold. Years later Robert Altman asked me to play a role in *Gosford Park*. When he told me who was in the cast I practically fainted, mostly because it included Michael.

Sadly, I was committed to another film from which I could not extricate myself and I still rue the day. When we finally did work together, I asked Michael about his experience on *Gosford Park* and he said it was wonderful.

Even though [in *Fortitude*] at that time he was using an ear-piece through which Milly would feed him his lines, his acting was impeccable. But I must admit that I did love it when the reception of the device would cut out from time to time, and he was unable to receive his next line. When this happened there would be a pause during which he would just stare at me. Then his huge hand would adjust the earpiece and in his booming voice he would say, 'Milly? I can't ... I can't hear you. Milly? Milly? Are you there? Where the hell are you?' He'd then look at me sheepishly and say, 'So sorry about this, darling.' Little did he know I would have waited for ever.

We filmed in freezing cold studios on an Icelandic glacier and we ate many meals together in our little hotel which fortunately had great food. During each of these meals he regaled us with stories of his extraordinary life and career, acted out other people's careers, and he and I discussed what we had seen that afternoon on our mutually favourite TV show, *Flog It!*

In Reykjavik, as we were heading back home to London after a couple of martinis, we ate our way through most of the delicious menu accompanied by a substantial amount of wine. Michael's company was, as always, joyous. That joyousness is what he gave to so many people through his work and to those of us who were fortunate enough to know him. It is that joyousness bound in his memory that I will hold in my heart for ever.

There was little to do on our rare days off and a five-minute walk from the hotel in Reyðarfjörður was a general store. It was more like a grand bazaar, with fur boots, bearskin coats, fishhooks, sun cream and husky treats, books on how to land a whale and manuals on hand-rearing puffins. Michael and I religiously made it a solemn pilgrimage to go to this shrine of commerce and spend as much as three euros on pairs of reading glasses and postcards for his boys, mainly of the spectacular Northern Lights, which we always managed to miss.

After our first visit to the shop through the six-foot tunnel of ice the owner had painstakingly created, we were surprised to find a queue of six little Icelanders aged between six and nine, each with a copy of Harry Potter and a shared biro.

Michael was wonderful and made them laugh by pulling faces and looking like Dumbledore by making a snowy beard and pulling the ear flaps up on his furry hat. After that, he would also buy little chocolate bars to reward the children, who somehow always magically appeared. We found it extraordinary how quickly they did so, until we began to suspect that the hotel receptionist and the storekeeper were in cahoots and later discovered they were all indeed related and our suspicions were justified.

34

'Never give in, never give in, never, never, never, in nothing, great or small, large or petty, never give in except to convictions of honour and good sense'

Michael was always generous with his fans, signing books. When we were on location for *Churchill's Secret*, lines of schoolchildren would form up having wandered in a crocodile past the set at Cliveden (standing in for Chartwell) only to stop, amazed, at seeing Dumbledore without his beard in a funny costume outside the house – clearly a time traveller. With whoops of joy they would surge down the hill separating the house from the gardens to meet their hero who, realising he had been discovered would, true to form, spring to his feet and greet them with his own almighty whoop of joy no matter how tired he was, completely rejuvenated.

Michael adored children because he always remained a child. He also always managed to sit up front with the pilot as we flew out to Reykjavik on several occasions and in blizzard conditions – shouting back to the terrified passengers that they were not to worry, he was taking over the controls as the pilot was a little drunk: 'It'll be fine!' He just loved mischief-making and couldn't help himself.

Churchill's Secret, filmed in June 2015, was a dramatisation of a little-known period in Churchill's life. In the summer of 1953, the prime minister suffered a life-threatening stroke, which was kept secret from the public. The film explored the physical and psychological struggle Churchill underwent as he tried to recover and at the same time battled the political machinations of those around him who want him to step down. It is a moving portrayal of the unwavering support he receives from his wife, Clementine (played by Lindsay Duncan), and his dedicated nurse Millie Appleyard (Romola Garai).

Michael, having been apprehensive at the start, thoroughly enjoyed working with director Charles Sturridge, and they formed a great collaboration. The cast and crew were amazing and incredibly supportive to Michael, who was feeling fragile at the time.

In 2015 came *Viceroy's House*, directed by Gurinder Chadha, which was an extraordinary experience, but one Michael struggled with.

It tells the story of Lord Mountbatten's arrival in 1947 as the last viceroy of India, tasked with overseeing the country's transition to independence. It depicts the complex political negotiations that led to the partition of India and Pakistan, and the human cost of the division. Michael played General Hastings Ismay, a pragmatist yet a complex character, deeply loyal to Mountbatten, who prioritised British interests and stability over the well-being of all Indians.

We spent a long time in Jodhpur and Rajasthan. The locations were spectacular, and we stayed in luxury at the Umaid Bhawan Palace, which is both a luxury hotel and the principal residence of the Jodhpur royal family.

Michael missed home, disliked the heat and the peacocks waking him at dawn, and struggled with the food. But at the same time there were many positives to the experience, and Michael especially loved having several old friends join the production as the cast included some erstwhile members of the RSC. We spent many happy evenings with Simon Williams and his wonderful wife, Lucy Fleming. We witnessed Holi, the sacred festival that gives Hindus and non-Hindus alike an opportunity to let off steam by throwing coloured water and powder at each other, an event he loved. He bought several handmade suits and had favourite shirts copied for an extremely reasonable price. Michael was also extremely fond of Gillian Anderson, Hugh Bonneville and Manish Dayal among his co-stars.

But Michael was also frightened, and he found the experience extremely stressful. He began to feel that foreign trips were too gruelling for him, he felt fragile, and he longed to be home. This was the first time I felt that 'the Great Gambon' might be deciding it was time for his curtain call. There were occasions when watching this mighty talent become bewildered and beset by fear was too heartbreaking. Nevertheless, he continued to give flashes of brilliance as well.

SIMON WILLIAMS

Michael Gambon and Simon Williams in conversation on the terrace of a palace in India – sunset. Here we would sit after the day's shooting had wrapped, looking out over the incredible

gardens and distant hills for a sundowner. Here is a typical example of their banter which kept Michael's spirits high.

sw: So, Michael . . . Why would you write this book – an
       autobiography?

mg: I'm not . . .

sw: Oh. Why not? Everyone will be very interested. All
       you've done, the people you've known, the places
       you've visited.

mg: It's none of their fucking business.

sw: They would pay you a shedload of money . . .

mg: [*His eyes brighten*] Wonga, huh? Hmm, well then . . .
       Warts 'n' All, that'll be the title.

———————————

Michael was extremely reliant on his agent Paul Lyon-Maris
and Independent Talent, and the team were hugely supportive
of him always. Their relationship spanned two decades, and
they were close friends as well as work colleagues. This was a
true collaboration and Michael trusted Paul's judgement and his
management skills as well as his advice. Whenever and wherever,
we worked, Michael would speak to Paul at least once a day, or
to Giacomo, his assistant.

PAUL LYON-MARIS

I had the honour of representing Michael for over twenty years . . .
he was a remarkable actor who was capable of transporting his
audience in ways that have been talked about and discussed
throughout this book . . . but he also had an ability of transforming moments in time into something magical and mischievous . . .

Every time I met Michael for lunch or dinner there was an event that impeded his ability to arrive on time . . . obviously he was just late . . . but his character could not allow such ordinary and mundane occurrences to pass by unembellished. One of the last times we met was at a restaurant in South Audley Street – he was over forty minutes late . . . on arrival he rushed over to the table – flustered and red-faced – with a story of how the taxi was held up at gunpoint and how the perpetrator tried to climb in through the window to snatch his wallet . . . he was channelling Dick Turpin and thought nothing of actually telling the story as if it was true (and maybe it was) even though some years before he had used the exact same excuse.

Another time he had witnessed a mugging and gone to the rescue of a young lady in distress, which accounted for his thirty-minute delay. All the time retelling with the smallest of details every moment of the experience.

Never one to under-embroider, he charmed and entertained throughout all our time together . . . forever enriching lives both on stage and off and in the many film and television productions . . . but also in everyday life . . . his storytelling was magnificent and I was enthralled throughout.

The effect was to make us all a little more aware of our surroundings and also our imaginations . . . to paint with our words so that those around have a richer experience.

35

'Don't go around speaking in that accent ... it's common'

It was becoming increasingly evident that Michael was not enjoying being on set and felt scared, and that every day was a struggle. It was devastating to watch this extraordinary man push himself on the set completely terrified and yet equally intoxicated, addicted at the thought of performing.

Dame Helen Mirren recalled towards the end of Michael's life how they discussed growing older and the positive effect that had on their work, in the richness and courage it brought, the fearlessness, full of feeling and of possibilities rather than conclusions.

Michael said that the older he got, the more Irish he felt, and told an interviewer: 'I feel at home in Dublin, although it's changed a lot. It's like every other bloody city now.'

On his last visit, Michael, who considered authenticity a personal affront, attended a grand function at Trinity College. Here he spent the entire evening channelling his Oirish accent and laid it on thick as peat. As he was about to leave, he was beckoned by one of the professors, who said gravely, 'Michael, please don't go around speaking in that accent.'

'Why not?' Michael asked, all wide-eyed innocence.

'It's common,' the professor answered solemnly.

Michael was thrilled, taking this as a compliment of epic proportions, and erupted into unrestrained laughter.

Although this third act in Michael's life was not always kind to the great knight, he often spoke about being King Lear. He always said that the madness appealed to him and that he somehow understood that. He recognised the turmoil and thought it must be like having dementia. When he goes out onto the heath, and he goes over the top.

Then his battle against his declining powers started to become overpowered by the wave of his increasing memory lapses. This was further exacerbated when his beautiful Airedale got dementia. The dog had reached twelve or thirteen and Michael was in agony about the dog's confusion and pain. The fact that he no longer recognised him. It frightened him and he would talk frantically about it as if that would keep it at bay.

Michael had met old people with dementia. He became haunted by the realisation that they intuited something was deeply wrong with them but couldn't quite put their finger on what it was.

Until one day, he would say with utter horror, the flashes back to consciousness stopped. In such moments, he would look utterly despairing, displaying his isolation and confusion as he felt set adrift amid the complexities of life. Much like one of the characters he inhabited for Beckett, he brilliantly conveyed the anxieties of old age, with its attendant incompetencies, bizarre rituals, deliberations and repetitions. Just as in *Krapp's Last Tape* so Michael would replay the tapes of his past, rewind a memory, then switch it off, punctuating his stories with a flash of Michael Colgan's production at Dublin's Gate Theatre or Olivier at the Old Vic, but most often he returned to Harold Pinter. It was unerring. There are so many ghosts, he would say, remembering his past heroes.

Judy, in 2018, was the last time we worked together, and it was painful. It was, like watching a moth batter itself against the light, unbearable.

The very last time I heard his incredible voice was over the phone.

'Mugwhay,' he said, 'it's all blurry. Where am I? Have you seen my stone? I've lost it, I can't find my stone.' It was his threnody against the destruction of his art.

'I go into a tunnel of nothingness like cotton wool. Is that when people are happier? When they become calm? What do you think when you enter the fog? Do you know? It is this, it is this, that I dread.'

In Beckett's *Krapp's Last Tape* the final words are spoken by the younger Krapp, reflecting on his past and the state of his present: 'Perhaps my best years are gone. When there was a chance of happiness. But I wouldn't want them back. Not with the fire in me now. No. I wouldn't want them back.'

EPILOGUE

It was lockdown, 2020. We were all prisoners of a kind, locked in our separate cells. And Michael was back in Kent, surrounded by his clocks, guns, cars and beloved workshop. The gates had closed, and my wonderful adventures as Sancho Panza to the great knight had ended, but I often think of him and thank him for the riches he brought to my life and to millions of others who will relive his brilliance for ever.

Michael died in Kent on 27 September 2023, aged eighty-two, following a bout of pneumonia.

Here is Tom and Will's farewell to their beloved father. A clarion call against ever forgetting those we love.

When Dad died, there were many wonderful tributes written by his friends and colleagues who described him as one of the finest stage actors of his generation, and it is clear that he was loved by many. We wanted to talk briefly about our memories of him as our father and the fun, love and laughter that we shared.

While Dad's loves were acting and everything mechanical – be it engineering, machine tools, his collection of eighteenth-century firearms, watches or cars – we have been told by many of his close friends that he loved becoming a father again in later life. All we know is that he gave us so much joy, fun, laughter and happiness and we hope and trust as children that we gave that back.

Our memories are that he was always happy to join in our games and dress up in various outfits, whatever we were into at the time. Be it a fireman, policeman, builder, or sailor, obviously this came quite naturally to him! Christmas was always a time for him to dress up in ridiculous outfits as well. He loved coming to our school and watching our various performances and recitals and our friends remember him giving a talk at our primary school with Dom West for support about playing Dumbledore, wearing a Gryffindor scarf and making everyone laugh, which the pupils loved. The teachers laughed more nervously as Dad told the children that he told lies to get the acting job he really wanted!

We had many tributes and lovely letters, including some from our teachers which showed Dad's interest in what we were doing and support for them. Will's old guitar teacher wrote that while most people knew him as the great actor he was, he just knew him as Will's dad who often chatted in his guitar lessons about the fun things they got up to on weekends and holidays. On reflection, Dad was probably mindful that he had left education at a young age, which he said wasn't a good thing. What he thought of our acting skills he kept to himself.

Most of the time, he was never happier than having a cup of tea and a cigarette at the café on the corner by our school, waiting for us to come out at the end of the day, and buying us a Mr Whippy ice cream, which was his favourite, from the van conveniently parked next to the playground.

In the summer, we would rent a house in Aldeburgh as our grandparents lived there, and he would enjoy going to the local pub with Grandpa and friends for a pint or two of bitter and getting fish 'n' chips on the way back. He always loved visiting the lifeboat station there and chatting with the crew who were on duty, and during carnival we were always made to watch the lifeboat team launching the boat into the sea, while standing on the beach, and putting money into buckets to help raise money for them. He was a man of habit, and it was obvious to us that he always enjoyed speaking to people who did manual things and were good with their hands.

Everyone seemed to enjoy Dad's company. He was always fun to be around, and he tried to put people at ease by making them laugh. Mum told us a story about Tom Felton, who played Draco Malfoy in Harry Potter, who had an intense scene with Dumbledore, and he kept forgetting his lines, so Dad pulled him aside saying, 'Do you know how much they're paying me? If you continue like this, I'll have a Ferrari by the end of the week, so keep it up.' Fart machines were always a favourite.

The tributes from his peers also showed his ability to find the fun in work, alongside being a dedicated professional, and his fellow actors obviously loved being in his company because of the laughter he generated. Well known for the games he'd start to play on other actors while on stage, particularly once he became bored with a long run …

Above all, he was gentle and kind, unless cigarettes ran out or milk and sugar for his tea. We always knew when he was arriving as the noise from the engine of his sports car could be heard from far away. When Tom was about two, Dad looked across to an empty seat, as he was in the footwell of his Audi R8, after driving around the local roundabout. Dad loved his cars, which Will seems to have inherited.

We always thought of him as wearing great clothes, whether in a crumpled linen suit or one from Savile Row. Mum said he resembled a modern-day version of Oscar Wilde in his big black overcoat, one of her velvet scarves that he always thought belonged to him, a wide-brimmed black fedora, and a lead in his hand with our pug Billy at the end of it.

He was great fun and brilliant with our friends and cousins, probably because Mum said he was a child at heart, and that all the best people are. Always the entertainer and joining in at every opportunity with us.

Lastly, Dad had a genuine love of animals, particularly with our pug dog in recent years who he liked to connect with when his speech was failing him, and he would reach out to both of us by making us laugh, even though things were difficult for him. We had known about his dementia for some time, even before Covid, which was an isolating and awful time for many, and particularly for those suffering from the disease. Once restrictions were lifted, we used to visit him most weekends, with a picnic, which he always enjoyed. Mum told us that he spoke about dementia in 2003 in relation to playing King Lear. When asked what he knew about the disease, he replied that he could just imagine it, which was always his approach to acting and to most things in life. He went on to say that eventually the person suffering from the disease disappears into a tunnel of nothingness, and he supposed that was when they were happier, and became quite calm. That brings us some comfort. We do know, however, that he has left us with wonderful memories, and he will always be much missed and loved by the two of us.

TOM and WILL HART GAMBON
December 2023

Acknowledgements

I am eternally indebted to the splendid and generous Richard Beswick at Little, Brown, who not only believed in this book but also provided invaluable support and guidance, including expert editing and the confidence to carry on. Also to the brilliant and talented team: Zoe Gullen and copy-editor Richard Collins, and to the design department.

Thanks to Stephanie Calman and Annabel Stacey who, despite their busy writing careers, read drafts and offered graceful suggestions and judicious advice. To Karin Van Der Werff and Constance de Vos for their stories and friendship. And the many cast and crew members who supported and helped Michael and me over the years.

Actors: Tom Hollander, Stanley Tucci, Dame Helen Mirren, Dame Eileen Atkins, Dame Judi Dench, Dame Penelope Wilton, Simon Callow, CBE, Dominic West, Simon Williams, Charles Dance, Lee Evans, Rufus Jones, Tim Ackroyd, Sir Ian McKellen, Lucy Fleming, Sir Derek Jacobi, John Standing, Sean Mathias, Simon Russell Beale, Ralph Fiennes, Bill Nighy, Dustin Hoffman, Robert De Niro, Al Pacino, Johnny Depp, Meryl Streep, Daniel Radcliffe, Daniel Craig, Matthew Macfadyen, Keeley Hawes, Brian Cox, Sir Michael Caine,

Kristin Scott Thomas, Sir Anthony Hopkins, Bob Stephens, John Stride, David Bradley, Phoebe Nicholls, David Walliams, Terence Rigby, Sir Tom Courtenay, Bill Sleigh, Charlotte Rampling, Joanne Whalley, Richard Bohringer, Dame Penelope Keith, Felicity Kendall, Christopher Eccleston, Gabriel Byrne, Simon McBurney, Romola Garai, Richard Dormer, Gillian Anderson, Hugh Bonneville, Manish Dayal, Lia Williams, Andrew Scott, Sir Kenneth Branagh, Jeremy Irons, Lindsay Duncan, Daisy Lewis, Bill Paterson, Barry McGovern, Justine Waddell, Greta Scacchi, Freddie Jones, Tim Roth, Gary Olsen, Ewan Stewart, Ciarán Hinds, Douglas Hodge, John Malkovich, David Thewlis, Hywel Williams-Ellis, Julia McKenzie, Monica Dolan, Abigail Lawrie, Timothy Spall, Miriam Margolyes, Malcolm Storry, Marlon Brando, Sir Ralph Richardson, Jack Lemmon, Sir Laurence Olivier, Dame Maggie Smith, Peter O'Toole, Pete Postlethwaite, Lady Olivier, Alan Rickman, Nicol Williamson, Richard Harris, Albert Finney, Dame Edith Evans, Alan Howard, Paul Scofield, Sir Antony Sher, Spike Milligan, Roger Lloyd Pack, Glenda Jackson, Natasha Richardson.

Directors: Eric Thompson, Harold Pinter, Sir Peter Hall, John Dexter, Peter Gill, Deborah Warner, Nicholas Hytner, Matthew Warchus, Rupert Goold, Alan Ayckbourn, Adrian Noble, Robert Altman, Tim Burton, Mike Nichols, Bill Gaskill, Charles Sturridge, Michael Mann, Gurinder Chadha, Patrick Marber, Alfonso Guarón, Robert De Niro, Henry Herbert, Nicholas Wright, Nicholas Renton, Elijah Moshinsky, Hilton Edwards, Micheál Mac Liammóir, Wes Anderson, Euzhan Palcy – and Peter Greenaway, for introducing Michael into my life.

Writers and playwrights: Harold Pinter, Lady Antonia Fraser, Samuel Beckett, Tom Stoppard, David Hare, Dennis

Potter, Alan Ayckbourn, J. K. Rowling, Nicholas Wright, Tony Kushner, Arthur Miller, Caryl Churchill, Bertolt Brecht, Andrew Davies, Peter Gill, Stephen Poliakoff, Simon Gray, Derek Walcott, Edward Albee, Christopher Hampton, Brian Friel.

Producers: Michael Colgan, Sonia Friedman, David Jonathan Heyman, Kees Kasander, Eric Fellner, Tim Bevan, David Yates.

Agents: Paul Lyon-Maris, Giacomo Palazzo, Harriet Robinson, Nina Gold, Sasha Robertson.

Especial and enormous thanks to Paul Lyon-Maris and Giacomo Palazzo and their team at Independent Talent for their generosity in putting me in touch with actors' agents, writers, producers and directors, without whose help I could not have started on this book. I also greatly appreciate working with you during my time with Michael on our many productions.

Thank you to Catherine Shoard for her excellent tribute, "'Delicate, dangerous, anarchic': Daniel Craig, Michael Mann, Matthew Macfadyen and more remember Michael Gambon', in the *Guardian*. Also Geraldine Bedell, Michael Owen, Elliot Levey, Oliver Soden, Philip Oakes and Michael Billington. Thank you, too, to David and Reynir from *Fortitude*, and to Andy Bottomley for his generous contribution of photographs.

A massive thank you to **Nick Hern,** for his huge generosity in allowing me to quote from *Michael Gambon: A Life in Acting* by Mel Gussow.

Finally, to my friends and family for making the world worth living in.

Your unwavering support and inspiration have been a constant source of strength and motivation, throughout this journey.

Lord Evgeny Lebedev, thank you for allowing me to sit in your house and write large chunks of it. To the entire company at Reschio, who housed, fed and hugely entertained me for two summers while I wrote a thousand letters: Contessa and Count Benedikt Bolza, Fiamma San Giuliano, Roger Granville and all the team. Sir Charles Forbes Adam and Rosalind, Lady Forbes Adam, for decades of support. Paola Moretti and Orso for their incredible hospitality. Richard McBrien and Dame Pippa Harris, Sophie Fiennes, Grainne Marmion, Eliza Poklewski Koziell, David and Annabel Stacey, Sabrina Guinness, Lord Peter Mandelson and Reinaldo Avila da Silva, Laraine Stokes, Emma Diamond, Andi Wright Lucinda Fouch, Richard Ellis and Chris Wyatt, who have all been pillars of strength through the years so generously offering their friendship, advice and belief, without which I would never have had the courage to start this.

And, of course, thank you to the GREAT GAMBON, for the many happy years we spent together on our adventures.

Sources

Extracts from *Michael Gambon: A Life in Acting* by Mel Gussow are reproduced with the kind permission of Nick Hern.

The recollections of Tom Hollander (pages ix, 9, 57, 75–6), Daniel Craig (page ix), Rupert Goold (pages 16, 121), Simon Callow (page 53), Dame Penelope Wilton (pages 58, 61–2), Matthew Warchus (pages 99–100), Michael Mann (page 110) and Matthew Macfadyen (pages 128–9) are from '"Delicate, dangerous, anarchic": Daniel Craig, Michael Mann, Matthew Macfadyen and more remember Michael Gambon' by Catherine Shoard, *Guardian*, 2 October 2023. Copyright Guardian News & Media Ltd.

Cindy Adams, *Lee Strasberg: The Imperfect Genius of the Actors Studio* (New York: Doubleday, 1980)

Paul Allen, *Alan Ayckbourn: Grinning at the Edge* (London: Methuen, 2001)

Alan Ayckbourn, *The Crafty Art of Playmaking* (London: Faber and Faber, 2002)

Geraldine Bedell, 'Behind the scenes', *Observer*, 29 February 2004. Copyright Guardian News & Media Ltd

Michael Billington, Alex Healey and Tom Silverstone, 'Cast

me as an actor with a funny walk: Michael Gambon
interviewed by Michael Billington – video', *Guardian*, 20
May 2014

'The Michael Billington archive: highlights from five decades
of reviews', *Guardian*, 20 December 2019

Karen K. Bradley, *Rudolf Laban* (Abingdon: Routledge, 2019)

Emma Brockes, 'Michael Gambon interview: Fail again, fail
better', *Guardian*, 28 June 2006

Darren Dalglish, 'Cressida', London Theatre, 8 June 2016

Declan Donnellan, *The Actor and the Target* (London: Nick
Hern Books, 2002)

Angie Errigo, '*Gosford Park* review', *Empire*, 1 January 2000

Antonia Fraser, *Must You Go? My Life with Harold Pinter*
(London: Weidenfeld & Nicolson, 2010)

'Harold Pinter by Michael Gambon and Tony Benn',
Independent, 27 December 2008

W. Stephen Gilbert, *The Life and Work of Dennis Potter* (New
York: Harry N. Abrams, 2002)

Mel Gussow, *Michael Gambon: A Life in Acting* (London:
Bloomsbury Academic, 2004; London: Nick Hern
Books, 2020)

Lyn Haill (ed.), *Olivier at Work: The National Years. Compiled
by the Royal National Theatre with Richard Olivier and Joan
Plowright* (London: Nick Hern Books, 1989)

'Michael Gambon remembered by David Hare', *Observer*, 21
December 2023. Copyright Guardian News & Media Ltd

Jim Hiley, *Theatre at Work: The Story of the National Theatre's
Production of Brecht's* Galileo (London: Routledge & Kegan
Paul, 1981)

David Jays, 'Michael Gambon: an actor who let his heart and
soul crack open', *Guardian*, 28 September 2023

Elliot Levey, 'The play that changed my life: "Michael Gambon's offstage anarchy as Falstaff made the show better"', *Guardian*, 15 July 2025

Jeremy Mailes, 'Rupert Goold of the Almeida Theatre', Plays International & Europe, 1 June 2020

Denise Martin, '"Harry Potter" countdown: Michael Gambon sees "no point" in reading Rowling's books', *Los Angeles Times*, 13 July 2009

Sheridan Morley, *A Talent to Amuse* (London: Penguin, 1974)

Jean Newlove and John Dalby, *Laban for All* (London: Nick Hern Books, 2004)

Bill Nighy on *This Cultural Life*, BBC Radio 4, 2 November 2024

Philip Oakes, 'Just between ourselves', *Telegraph*, 10 February 1990

Laurence Olivier, *Laurence Olivier in His Own Words* (London: Penguin/BBC Studios Distribution Ltd, 2022)

Harold Pinter, 'Art, Truth and Politics: The Nobel Lecture', in *Various Voices: Sixty Years of Prose, Poetry, Politics 1948–2008* (London: Faber & Faber, 2013)

Antony Sher, *Beside Myself: An Actor's Life* (London: Hutchinson, 2001)

Oliver Soden, 'The unforgettable Michael Gambon', *Engelsberg Ideas*, 26 September 2024

Mark Taylor-Batty, *The Theatre of Harold Pinter* (London: Bloomsbury Methuen Drama, 2014)

'Alan Rickman & Helena Bonham Carter interview for "Harry Potter and the Deathly Hallows – Part 2", via The [AR]chive, 7 July 2011.

'Q and A with Michael Gambon, Professor Albus Dumbledore in Harry Potter', Futuremovies.co.uk, 5 July 2007

RAISING READERS
Books Build Bright Futures

Dear Reader,

We'd love your attention for one more page to tell you about the crisis in children's reading, and what we can all do.

Studies have shown that reading for fun is the **single biggest predictor of a child's future life chances** – more than family circumstance, parents' educational background or income. It improves academic results, mental health, wealth, communication skills, ambition and happiness.[1]

The number of children reading for fun is in rapid decline. Young people have a lot of competition for their time. In 2024, 1 in 10 children and young people in the UK aged 5 to 18 did not own a single book at home.[2]

Hachette works extensively with schools, libraries and literacy charities, but here are some ways we can all raise more readers:

- Reading to children for just 10 minutes a day makes a difference
- Don't give up if children aren't regular readers – there will be books for them!
- Visit bookshops and libraries to get recommendations
- Encourage them to listen to audiobooks
- Support school libraries
- Give books as gifts

There's a lot more information about how to encourage children to read on our website: **www.RaisingReaders.co.uk**

Thank you for reading.

---

[1] OECD, '21st-Century Readers: Developing Literacy Skills in a Digital World', 2021, https://www.oecd.org/en/publications/21st-century-readers_a83d84cb-en.html

[2] National Literacy Trust, 'Book Ownership in 2024', November 2024, https://literacytrust.org.uk/research-services/research-reports/book-ownership-in-2024